Sinéad Stubbins is a writer, editor and cultural critic in Melbourne. She made her name writing TV recaps for *Junkee* on shows such as *The Bachelor* and *Game of Thrones*, and she's also on the writing team for *The Weekly with Charlie Pickering* on ABC. She has written for *The Guardian*, *The Saturday Paper*, *frankie*, *The Big Issue*, *New York Magazine* and many other publications – mainly about pop culture, friendship and the embarrassing moments that you think about in the five minutes before you go to sleep.

Photo by Amelia Dowd

IN MY DEFENCE

I HAVE NO DEFENCE

Published by Affirm Press in 2021
28 Thistlethwaite Street, South Melbourne,
Boonwurrung Country, VIC 3205
affirmpress.com.au
10 9 8 7 6 5 4 3 2 1

Title: In My Defence I Have No Defence / Sinéad Stubbins, author
ISBN: 9781922419194 (paperback)

 A catalogue record for this
book is available from the
NATIONAL LIBRARY OF AUSTRALIA National Library of Australia

Cover design by Design by Committee
Typeset in 12.5/20.5 Adobe Garamond Premier Pro by J&M Typesetting
Proudly printed in Australia by Griffin Press

 The paper this book is printed on is certified against the
Forest Stewardship Council® Standards. Griffin Press holds
chain of custody certification SGSHK-COC-005088. FSC®
promotes environmentally responsible, socially beneficial
and economically viable management of the world's forests

IN MY DEFENCE

I HAVE NO DEFENCE

Sinéad Stubbins

Affirm press

Contents

You know that feeling of gentle contentment, that calm and present energy that materialises when you know in every miraculous cell of your body that you can trust yourself completely? That surge of moral fortitude coursing through your veins like an electric current, grounding your feet to the pulsating earth like some ancient, dignified tree?

Well I have never felt that once in my whole fucking life; you'll have to tell me what it's like some time.

Maybe you feel great just the way you are. I'm happy for you, truly. *I really am very happy for you; it's true, I honestly could not be happier for you, I mean truly.* Maybe you got that way from mindfulness, or cupping your hands around a ceramic mug of ginger tea while slowly breathing in salty air and listening to the swell of the sea, or from not being Catholic, or from bullet journalling on your lunch break, or ironing vast swathes of linen, or listening to a specific podcast episode featuring Brené Brown. Brené Brown probably hears the sea wherever she goes. Her linen probably doesn't even crease.

This book isn't about finding yourself. I'm sorry if that's the kind of beach read you were after. It's about having found yourself and then strategising with all the solemn concern of a moustachioed World War I battle captain (you know, one of the ones on the winning side) ways to make that self more palatable to other humans. 'Onwards, men!' you say, except to your own brain.

It's about being uncomfortable in your own skin and wanting to try someone else's skin on for size (is that what *Silence of the Lambs* is about, please don't tell me).

It's about wishing you could call *Renovation Rescue* on your personality, except you can't because Scott Cam would just turn up with his Phillips head screwdriver like, 'Ah, what can I even do here?' and in any case that show ended in 2006.

It's about that sneaking suspicion that you're not doing it right, perhaps triggered by the realisation that you're closer to Sandy Cohen's age than Seth Cohen's.

It's about that time in 1999 when my classmate Fran made a burn book about every girl in our class, and in between calling one girl a 'slut' (she had boobs) and another 'boring' (she was), she accused me of being a 'try-hard'. 'It's only because you try *so hard* at everything you do,' said my popular sort-of friend Anna-Grace tactfully, when the principal made us go around the room to refute each other's burn-book accusations. The other girls nodded sympathetically. Anna-Grace was lying. This book is about try-hards.

Have I lost you? Let's press on anyway. I deeply feel in every crevice of my jealous, depraved heart that I could achieve a better and more perfect model of myself if I just focused *a bit harder*.

That if I listened to the right song, or won the right (any) literary award, or followed the right Instagram psychologist, or drank kombucha, ever, or enacted the correct seventy-step Korean skincare regime, I would achieve it.

At the time of writing this, there is a list in my diary of people who I want to be better friends with. I wrote this list at an insecure moment when it felt imperative to create a more social version of myself: a version who might receive texts that said, *Hey want to come to this thing?* and reply, *Cool, see you in 20*, and who only felt shame when it was appropriate, and who had many different friends in many different cities, especially people who were Twitter-famous and would tweet about a funny thing I had said and invite me to strange openings where they would take hilarious photos of me gesticulating hilariously at artwork.

'Are you … very social, though?' a psychologist asked me, eyebrow arched, when I told her of my plan.

'No,' I said. 'But wouldn't it be better if I was?'

Maybe it would be better and maybe it wouldn't, but it's worth a try. And I really do try hard at everything I do.

The body

'An apple a day keeps the doctor away, but you
could eat five hundred apples and you still
wouldn't know what jeans to buy or what fitness
class you should be taking. They're just apples.
I don't know what to tell you.'

—*A man, 1913*

Java junkie

You're waiting in line to buy a $4.50 filter coffee that costs extra because the beans come from Brazil (the only other type of beans available don't have a listed country of origin so maybe they're beans from Bunnings or maybe they're just small rocks). That doesn't matter right now, because this ritual – buying an expensive, hot coffee on a blustery, foggy morning, the kind of morning that makes you think of *Little Women* and Christmases spent around a fire and scarlet fever – is a luxury, a moment for you, a fail-safe excuse to shave exactly six minutes off the start of your workday.

'Sorry I'm late – I'm just a java junkie!' you might say when you walk in at 9.06am, with a wink to your workmates, who hate you.*

---

* You wish you were *actually* the kind of person who could arrive six minutes late to work without dying of shame. Imagine being that person? Imagine being so confident that you could swan in at 9.06am, assume that everyone knows you tried your best to arrive on time and not blurt out, 'SORRY, THE TRAM!' as soon as you see your workmates, who didn't even notice that you were six minutes late anyway. For the rest of the day, you're compelled to compulsively splutter, 'THE TRAM!' in every meeting to explain your tardiness. You stay at the office fifty minutes later than everyone else to repent.

You wonder what would happen if you started walking around the office with an empty coffee mug saying things like 'Cold one today!' or 'Get up to much on the weekend?' or alternatively, on Wednesdays, 'I'm just hanging out for Friday, how about you?' You wonder if you should become one of those people who walks up to people's desks, talks to them about nothing for five minutes and then says, 'Anyway! Didn't have anything to ask, just visiting,' and then wanders away while everyone in the office is imagining what it would feel like to hold you down and stab you with a fine liner.

'Ah, like Sinéad O'Connor?' the cafe's cashier says when you give him your name, which you don't mind because it means that he actually identifies your name as a human name. You won't get 'Shanae' or 'Sinid' or 'Shanny' this day! You won't even need to use 'Andy', your boyfriend's name, which is what you sometimes do to avoid confusion and to move through the world with the ease of an Andy. Your mum always said that if you didn't remember to write the accent in your name it meant that you were not spelling it correctly. She didn't consider that no one in Australia would be able to spell or pronounce it with or without the accent. 'What a strange name!' baristas will tell you until you die. 'What a strange name!' the priest conducting your funeral will say as your corpse is lowered into the dirt. Recently at a birthday dinner, a drunk Baby Boomer asked you, 'Do you really have a funny line in your name, or did you add that in to make yourself seem more interesting?' You can't deny that this is exactly the kind of thing that you would do. You never get to answer her anyway, because another Baby Boomer at the table interrupts and says, 'Sinéad, do you think the #MeToo movement has gone too far?'

The cashier's eyes linger on you for a moment longer than necessary and he smiles. You avoid his eye and shuffle to the side of the cafe.

A toddler waddles up to the cafe counter holding a credit card. His mum thinks it's funny for the toddler to pay for their meal, because the idea of a baby owning a credit card is funny. In fact, you know lots of financially irresponsible people who have the emotional capacity of babies, and they're allowed credit cards. Does this baby know about current interest rates? Does this baby know that the casual use of a credit card – the everyday purchases, the ones you don't think about – is what gradually crushes you under the leaden weight of debt?

Not long ago at a pub, a toddler waved at you and your friends, and your friends waved back, and then the toddler threw his water bottle at you, smashing a wine glass and showering you in broken shards. The toddler's parents (who were both wearing fisherman's pants, which isn't relevant but sort of is) said, 'Oh no!' to the baby, didn't acknowledge you, then walked out of the pub while you shook broken glass off your hands. Another time, you were sitting in the food court at Chadstone, and a baby walked up to you and your sister, and you said, 'Hello!' and then the baby held eye contact with you for a second, raised her baby-fist and punched you once, hard, in the chest. Just yesterday, in another pub, your friend flung her baby at you and you started yelling, 'WHICH BIT DO I HOLD UP?' and she waved her hand dismissively, and you just crossed your hands and pressed him to your chest, and his whole face was smooshed against your collarbone and he was frowning, and all of your friends laughed and took photos of you failing from different angles. You wonder how a baby who didn't have the ability to eat solid foods somehow had the ability to be exasperated with you.

The toddler taps the credit card on the cafe's EFTPOS machine. Everyone in the cafe laughs.

Standing beside you is a man with shoulder-length brown hair that is held down by a five-panel cap. The cap is advertising an indie book publisher that mostly publishes zines. You wonder if the man feels passionate about zines or just likes hats. He glances at you, looks away and glances back. He takes his full KeepCup and leaves. A gust of cold air rushes in when he exits. A blonde woman sitting at a table reading her phone through large, black-rimmed glasses looks up momentarily, stares at you then looks down at her phone again. It's only when a couple who are waiting to pay – each covered head-to-toe in long puffer jackets that must be too warm for a Melbourne winter – both look you square in the face that something *bings*, like a notification sent directly to your brain.

People keep looking at you this morning. Like, *really* looking at you. Something is happening here. You're not famous on

Instagram, so it has to be something else. You play with a loose thread on your sturdy, unflattering workman's pants.

Wait ... you think. Am I beautiful?

Is it possible that I am beautiful? Is it possible that I have been beautiful this whole time and never noticed?

Once, when you were nineteen, a woman who said she was in 'modelling' did approach you on Bourke Street and gave you her card, but you think that she probably just needed someone who looked like a sickly twelve-year-old – maybe for an RACV drunk-driving commercial; maybe you'd play a child cyclist who died. Did *she* know you were beautiful? Have you wasted your whole life acting with the apologetic smallness of an unattractive person? Should you have been giving speeches and taking part in gymnastics competitions and working in high-end retail and going to the beach, *this whole time*?

Your name is called and you smile at the barista with the self-assurance of a beautiful person. Your life has changed. Things will be different for you now. You wonder if you should ask for a promotion today. You wonder if you should ask for a pay rise. You wonder if doors will be held open for you wherever you go. You wonder if your boyfriend will go wild with jealousy whenever bartenders give you free drinks. You wonder if you should take your Instagram off private.

You walk onto the street with a burning-hot coffee cup (you should be punished for forgetting your KeepCup; asking for a double cup is basically admitting you're a right-wing climate-change-denier) and a new lease on life as you head to your office across the road. You press the code to open the door and catch your reflection in the glass.

A small pool of dark blood had accumulated at the base of your bottom lip. It is connected to a thin red line that traces up inside your mouth. It reminds you of in movies when someone accidentally ingests poison and suddenly starts coughing up blood bubbles because their insides are fighting to get out. Their eyes go wide like they're trying to say, 'Wait, my body doesn't usually feel like this,' then they collapse and die. You don't think that anyone could have snuck you poison this morning. Besides, you don't know any life-ruining secrets about powerful businessmen and you're not the heir to any large fortune, so why would they want to? The most expensive thing you own is a *Seinfeld* DVD box set and no one wants that. You feel fine. But why is there blood?

While preparing to make peace with your imminent death, you lick the corner of your mouth, and instead of the metallic taste of blood, you get the metallic taste of a red pen that has burst on your lip when you touched it to your face in a performative show of contemplation on the tram an hour earlier. You were writing a list of things to be grateful for. Ironically, *I'm not bleeding from the face* didn't make the list. You spit on the side of your hand and rub it off, leaving an angry red mark on your face.

'Did you eventually figure out that you had blood coming out of your mouth yesterday?' the cafe cashier may say tomorrow,

12

keeping his distance like it's some new plague. Maybe you should never go to that cafe again. Maybe you should start going to an identical one that is one block further away from work. You will walk in, cheeks aflame in a good way from the whip of Melbourne's winter winds. You will unfurl yourself from your large scarf, which is clean and not covered in blood, and approach the counter, breathless. 'Name?' the barista will ask, texta poised on your future coffee cup.

'Andy,' you will say, with a smile.

Rebel rebel

We all have catchphrases. These are things that we say with such regularity that it's as if they have been scripted for us – like saying, 'Sick one,' when something goes well or, 'Ah, sugar,' when something goes badly or, 'What's the damage?' when the bill arrives and you're pretending not to be frightened.

One of my very favourite things in life is saying, 'I don't mind, I trust you!' in a high voice, usually while someone is bleaching great chunks of my hair or tearing wax strips off my brow bone with such ferocity that my eyelid threatens to detach from my face. This attitude, this cursed 'I don't mind, I trust you!' attitude, is the reason why I have never left a hairdresser with a haircut that I actually like.* I am a genius at this. I am an absolute genius at paying someone $120, not showing them the reference picture of Alexa Chung I have saved on my phone and saying, 'I don't mind, I trust you!' – which it turns out is

---

* Since writing this I have found a hairdresser that I like. I don't want to officially announce the relationship in case she breaks up with me.

14

hairdresser for 'Some sort of mushroom shape with a fringe that looks like it's crawling back up into my skull, thanks.'

And yet, I persist. Perhaps there is a 'new me' around the corner, waiting for the right haircut or facial injection before she emerges. Maybe I can put one of those acid-peel things on my face, and when I peel it off I'll look like Elizabeth Taylor (pre-old). Maybe if I eat an orange while applying vitamin-C serum to my skin, some miraculous chemical reaction will take place and I will look moist enough to kiss, but not so moist that I need to be hosed down.

Aside from reasons of beauty, making aesthetic renovations often feels imperative when you want to convey something about your deviant identity, but don't fully trust that your actual personality will be able to do that for you. Maybe it's getting a massive Black Flag tattoo on your belly. Maybe it's growing a mullet so everyone knows you'd hate to work in a bank. For me, it was always about proving to people that despite whatever ordinary setting they found me in, I was different. I wanted everyone who looked at me to think I was rebellious – I *longed* for it. Rules? *Pfft.* They're not for me, man. I'd rather die than conform to your mainstream ideals. I'm an oddball.

I tried to prove this by getting my ears pierced.

I wasn't allowed to get my ears pierced until I turned fifteen, at which point I decided that it wasn't cool to get your ears pierced because it meant that you cared about how you looked (or at least that was the story I was sticking to – my dad had an earring and I don't think I wanted to give him the satisfaction of knowing that I did actually find him to be quite rebellious).

After many years of wearing backwards baseball caps and then feeling this wasn't actually conveying the insurgent energy I was going for, at the age of twenty-nine I decided it was time to do something more radical. In retrospect, the timing was not coincidental. I had suddenly reached an alarmingly conventional period of life: I lived with my partner of six years in a small apartment and we often had vegetables in the fridge. I was working at a big advertising company (full-time!) where I mainly sense-checked copy for alcohol brands. My dad had worked in construction and my mum was a nurse, and my job was checking if 'whisky' or 'whiskey' was more correct in the context of an Instagram post.

'You look professional!' a colleague said to me one day, as I was walking into a client meeting. It felt as though she had picked up her stapler and shot a piece of jagged metal directly through my heart. I wasn't working a particularly creative job at the time, so no one in my life was asking, 'So – what's next for you?' with a pitying glance over a glass of oaky chardonnay that they could afford and I couldn't. I knew I should have been grateful about that but I wasn't, not all the time anyway. I wasn't writing much. I wasn't bothering with Twitter and didn't always know about gross videos that my extremely online friends would mention in conversation. Everything was stable. I needed to poke a hole in my flesh.

'What a weird decision!' one of my colleagues said to me when I disclosed my plans. 'Like, why now? You're a weird age to be suddenly doing that?'

I smiled a smug smile. I could tell she thought I should be embarrassed. But I wanted to be the sort of person who made *super weird* decisions. The active and unnecessary nature of the activity appealed to me. I was pretending that I wanted the piercings because I found them aesthetically pleasing, when really I just thought it would make me look cooler to other people – something you should never admit to, because it's very uncool.

Now, I know that getting a piercing (in your *ear* no less – not your tongue or eyebrow or lip or belly button or nipple or butt, if that's possible) is about as rebellious as a 1950s anti-vandalism PSA. *Why didn't she shave her hair off?* you might be thinking. I couldn't do that because Sinéad O'Connor had already done that, and I couldn't stand discussing it with every gen Xer I encountered until it grew out. *What about tattoos?* you might suggest. Actually, I already had two small stick-and-poke tattoos on my left arm, which was basically the least rebellious thing you could do in Melbourne. They pretty much stick-and-poked you the first time you tried to top up your Myki card.

So it had to be a piercing.

Despite recommendations from chic workmates about studios that 'designed your ear' for you – like your ear was a dull enclave that needed a few throw rugs and a mid-century modern end table – I made an appointment at a cheaper, but still clean and respectable beauty centre for my piercing the next day.

When I arrived I was directed to a white room that was full of soft cream furniture trimmed in pink and gold, like a fancy spa, or heaven. As I sat on a table that was covered in a crisp white sheet, I noticed a lot of framed posters of blonde children with pierced ears, all with the same vacant and vaguely self-satisfied expression. In one of the posters, the vacant smiling blonde child was wearing a small crown and holding a large hand, perhaps leading her to a fancy toddler convention or her first investment property. In another, a smiling blonde baby was sitting in someone's adult arms, tiny silver earrings wedged in her tiny baby lobes. I had never seen a more condescending baby in all my life. All the furniture around me suddenly seemed very small, and I realised that I had been put in the 'keep crying kids calm while we jam a needle in their ear, they'll thank us later' room.

'I want to use a needle, if possible,' I said confidently to the piercer when she began swabbing my lobes. A fancy girl at work had told me that a needle produces cleaner and more sophisticated results than a gun, and I believed her because she always knew about things like that (she had recently taught me what a sheet mask was). As an older woman, I needed to know these things. I knew things those babies *just didn't know.*

The piercer frowned. 'Ah ... why do you want a needle?' she said, with a look of incredulity, as if I had asked her to pierce my ear with a shard of diamond or a carrot.

'Don't worry!' I said in a high voice, ashamed.

She proceeded to gun my ears, the only sound in the room the *pee-chaw!* of the machine. I didn't resist. I was new to this subculture after all.

This satisfied me for a few months, but soon a familiar longing crept back in – the longing to do something super weird. I wondered if turning thirty had flipped a new switch of insecurity in my brain. I knew I wasn't old, but I didn't feel *young*-young anymore. There were suddenly apps I didn't understand but I wasn't buying a house or trying to get a promotion, and I got too mad at posters of babies to ever consider having a real one myself. I needed to show how restless I felt, to prove that my identity still had the capacity for aesthetic spontaneity. I needed a stranger to punch another hole in my ear for no reason.

'I've just decided this minute that I'm going to get more piercings tonight!' I said to people at my new advertising job, who smiled politely while I showed them reference images of Instagram women with multiple gold hoops. This time I didn't make an appointment at a light-filled beauty salon with delicate studs on display – my rebellion had a ticking clock on it. I went to the only place that would take me after work: a waxing and piercing chain (what a one-stop ouchy shop!) housed in the dark underground level of a shopping centre in the CBD.

The shopfront was decorated with the sort of aggressive, jagged graffiti that Year Eights draw on their school books. Fifteen minutes after I'd arrived, my name was called.

'I only got my ears pierced for the first time last year!' I said to the piercer, for some reason.

'Oh, really?' she said sweetly. I realised I had expected her to be surprised. I wondered how many insecure thirty-year-olds in advertising she had pierced that day.

Now that I was sitting down on the plastic chair covered by a transparent plastic sheet, I could see that this person was at least ten years younger than me, maybe more. She wore heavy eyeliner, had dead-straight hair and there was a big tattoo on her arm dedicated to someone who I assumed had either been born or died in 2006. 'That was the year I graduated high school!' I almost said, but didn't say.

The piercer asked where I wanted my second piercings, and I admitted that I was suddenly quite stressed about the exact location, not knowing how far away it should be from my original set.

'You decide, I trust you!' I said, to which she shrugged and got to work.

I wondered how ridiculous I seemed to her. In less than a minute she had not only pierced both my ears, but managed to do so while having a yelling conversation with the girl at reception about the shopping centre's new opening hours. It was impressive multitasking to say the least.

Guess what I just did, I wrote to a group chat of my friends, hoping to shock them.

It was a few days before I realised the desperation of what I had done – effectively, a much more embarrassing version of chucking on a pink polo shirt, slicking my hair back with pomade, buying a Porsche and sleeping with my secretary. Engaging in some sort of age-related crisis that involved me wearing large bolt studs for six weeks and wincing every time I accidentally touched my earlobes. This wasn't weird in a good way. It wasn't actually anything. Had I really thought that a new ear hole would make me feel better?

This wasn't the first time I had failed to perfectly perform what I considered my 'true' rebellious identity. Even as an actual teenager I couldn't get it right. When I was sixteen, my family went to Ireland, which was significant because we were not the kind of family who ordinarily took trips overseas: my parents had only gone back to Ireland for funerals, and my siblings and I had only been out of Victoria once or twice.

It was a trip packed with family visits played out in cigarette-smoke-filled stone cottages. In my dad's hometown of Effin (yes) we rented a house that was next to a church. From my bedroom window, I could see a full-size statue of Jesus nailed to the cross (I would say 'to scale' but I don't know if he really was that tall). One night, having finally fallen asleep after trying not to think about dying Jesus judging me, I was shaken awake by an older woman, peering at me through huge round glasses in the dark. She told me she was my great aunt and that she just wanted to say hello.

'Next time you come back, I'll probably be dead,' she whispered, before patting me on the head and shuffling out of the room.

When we travelled to Dublin, another great aunt handed me a fistful of euros. I was amazed at my sudden wealth and immediately started strategising ways to avoid sharing it with my siblings. I used some of the money to buy sneakers with cherries on them and then headed to the HMV superstore. As I flicked through a rack of black band tees that mostly depicted the Ramones, I gasped when I found a shirt featuring one of my hard-rock obsessions. I had bought their CD the year before and my mum had frowned at the photo of the bare butt on the back cover. The band's baby tee was black with silver foil lettering and, in my estimation, made me look more or less exactly like Joan Jett. I took the tee and my dodgy cash straight to the counter.

As soon as my mum saw me bounding down the street with shopping bags, the jig was up. 'They don't even know what to do with money!' I protested, as she watched me split the remainder of the notes into my brother's and sister's small, outstretched hands.

At the end of the holiday we spent a couple of days in Rome visiting another great aunt (if you have Irish parents, you will have approximately ten to twelve great aunts). One day was set aside for a visit to the Vatican. 'We can see the Pope!' my mum said, and I knew that she meant the Dead Pope and not the

Living Pope. Pope John Paul II had died on the morning that we left Australia to travel to Ireland, which in retrospect was a very bad omen. His dead body was still on display when we arrived in Rome, though, so timing-wise it worked out quite well. In the lead-up to the visit, I thought carefully about the dramatic ways I could refuse to attend, purely with the aim of annoying my mum. If Sinéad O'Connor could tear up a picture of the Pope on *Saturday Night Live* – something I never saw, but had read about – I could support the legacy of our shared name in a similarly dynamic way. The Vatican represented the old world: old customs, old rules, old binaries that I wanted my parents to know I opposed. I wasn't sure on what grounds I opposed them, but it felt good to say that I did.

My mum frowned that morning when I came out of my room wearing my black band T-shirt but didn't say anything, as if she knew that commenting on the choice would give me too much satisfaction. In my shocking, positively vulgar shirt, I posed for photos with my brother and sister, the three of us standing in the same formations as all the other hundreds of tourists in St Peter's Square. The line to see the Dead Pope was too long, so we went and got gelati instead.

In one of the photos, my brother Ciarán and I are smiling, squinting through the glare, small figures beneath the towering obelisk from the Circus of Nero. Ciarán, tiny and in a red hat that was specifically bought so we wouldn't lose him in a crowd, is sweetly giving the peace sign. I have my arms over my head, as if I am stepping onstage at the end of a successful performance of *Gypsy*. The silver 'The Darkness' logo on my T-shirt glints in the sun.

The thing is, deep down in my increasingly aged guts, I know that being a real rebel has nothing at all to do with how many holes you've poked in your body, or the crap band on your baby tee, or having a Mohawk so tall that it gives the impression you have recently been electrocuted (although, that is very cool, I have to say). Making bold aesthetic statements can make you feel more like yourself, or part of a tribe, or signal that you're refusing to hide a part of yourself that society has told you is wrong – those things aren't as superficial, because they're authentic. Real rebellion isn't so predictable.

Real rebellion is the teenage girl I saw in Melbourne's Treasury Gardens the other day, who had a sign that said, *Compost the bourgeoisie*; and the tiny gentleman in a trilby hat with a placard that said, *Thanks for ruining my life, ScoMo, you idiot*; and the group of five elderly ladies with canes carrying around a placard that said, *Grandmas for climate action*. I found it all so moving that I cried like a baby on and off for about two hours (behind my sunglasses – I wasn't going to tell on myself in front of these cool children). My large starter studs and I were shamed.

At the time of writing this, enough weeks have passed that I can take out the obnoxious studs and replace them with a more subtle, chic hoop from Chemist Warehouse. It's a pretty big achievement, and I'm glad I've made it this far. I am admiring them in the mirror, enjoying the glint of the earrings as I turn my head. I am enjoying the extra weight they bring to my ears. I am wondering if when people see them in bars or on trams, they will think I am confident and unruly, and assume I know how to ride a skateboard. I wonder if they will think they're super weird.

Dancing

As a kid I did jazz ballet for approximately four months before I realised it was taking up the time I could have used doing nothing, so I gave it up. My little sister, Monica, and my brother, Ciarán, did swimming and played T-ball, and Monica even had a brief stint going to Sunday School-esque day camps. (Her friends were doing it, which I'm pretty sure is the only reason she did. She doesn't seem any more Catholic than Ciarán or I in any case.)

I think my parents were proud that two of their children did extracurricular activities, because it sounded very wholesome. 'Yeah, I just took the kids to swimming this morning,' I imagined them saying to other parents, parents who wore Country Road jumpers, drove four-wheel drives and worked in finance. I don't think they had friends like this, but I imagined that they did*.

---

* I can't remember my dad ever hanging out with parents from school. My dad's best stories usually involve explaining really bad things (getting beaten up, the IRA, cousins marrying each other, people getting stabbed with a

26

There was something about extracurricular activities that felt so Australian to me. I wondered what it would be like to be one of those kids who were hypnotised by the rising sun and, in a trance, got up at 6am, put on cricket whites and dutifully took part in physical activities on manicured lawns. Those kids probably watched *Home and Away* instead of *Ballykissangel.* They ate Vegemite. I wondered if they even knew what soda bread was. I felt sorry for them.

Nothing felt more wholesome – more right – than when both my siblings took up Irish dancing. It was as if they were making up for all my social deficiencies, like I was some sort of cultureless gremlin child who stayed indoors with the curtains drawn while my long-limbed siblings yearned to leap into the fresh air. Monica still maintains that she was crap at Irish dancing (we all remember Ciarán being great at it, although he was probably just average and made up for a lack of talent by being an adorable blond six-year-old jumping around to jangle music) but I knew that acquiescing to do it meant much more than being good at it. My mum rented Monica long-sleeved dresses covered in Celtic crosses. (Years before this, my mum had a Communion dress made for me that had a pink Celtic cross embroidered into the waist. Irish parents seem sure of two things: a Celtic cross can jazz up any outfit, and singing

---

sword) in a really funny way that is sometimes jarring for non-Irish people. Australian parents rarely tell stories about swords, so maybe my dad didn't bother interacting with them much.

'Fairytale of New York' out loud makes doing the dishes feel quicker.) She also bought Monica a clip with cascading ringlets of fake hair that all the Irish dancing girls wore on their ponytails, so when they jumped the fake curls also jumped, like they were on a rollercoaster.

One time, Monica fell off the monkey bars and broke her foot, but no one believed her so she had to go to Irish dancing anyway. Maybe her teachers were impressed by the anguish on her face and thought it was centuries of ancestral trauma working its way out. Recently my boyfriend asked me if there is a cultural reason why Irish dancing involves denying yourself the use of your arms – was it a metaphor for powerlessness in the face of British imperialism? 'Yes,' I said, and then refused to elaborate because I couldn't be bothered looking up what it actually was.

One St Patrick's Day, when my cousin Niamh was in primary school, one of her teachers asked her if she would like to do some Irish dancing at assembly. Niamh didn't actually know how to do Irish dancing, but my aunty thought it was a great idea. She knew the basic gist – hands by the sides, stick one leg out and then another and just hop between the two. We were Irish, after all. We just *knew*.

On the morning of the assembly, a teacher said to Niamh, 'Guess what, you're going to dance with a partner!' It turned out that the other girl was actually a trained Irish dancer who went to classes on the weekend. Niamh was just Irish and had legs. They stood side-by-side and the music started to play. The dancer girl began to move in time with the music. Niamh tried to copy her, hopping on alternate feet and springing up as high as she could. She wasn't asked to perform again.

The Code

Oh, you've been invited to an event? Well, aren't you the belle of the ball. I expect Mr Darcy will ask you to dance, right there in front of everyone. I bet you and Cha Cha, the best dancer at St Bernadette's, will set the floor aflame with your rendition of the 'hand-jive'. I imagine you'll be taken home in Theodore Laurence's carriage after you twist your ankle. Oh, how the debutantes will gossip about a man's *hands* touching your *naked* and *exposed* and *sexual ankle*. Well, *aren't we special.*

But oh wait, the dress code is 'cocktail' so maybe you shouldn't go at all. The stress involved in ascertaining the correct interpretation of 'cocktail' will far outweigh any fun you could possibly have at this event. Even if it's your best friend's birthday party. Even if it's *Oprah's* birthday party.

For quite some time now – or, at least, for as long as I have been aware of the dress code 'cocktail' (which happens at around twenty-four, the same time that you realise that the thing you wanted to be in high school isn't really the thing you want to be now and, oh god, why did I do all that *studying* and, uh oh, people around me sure seem keen on entering Serious Relationships, is this the time we're meant to be doing that, because I sort of thought – wait, what are you saying, the reason that my skin is spotty and my hair is falling out is because I don't drink water, *WHO KNEW ABOUT WATER?* It's a time of hard revelations) I have sort of concluded that 'cocktail' is a scam.

I have this persistent suspicion that whoever invented the cocktail dress code (King Edward VIII, prior to abdicating? The Baroness in *The Sound of Music*? One of the Heathers in *Heathers*?) did so in order to weed out the less-than-ideal people in their lives: the ones who aren't quite sophisticated enough to fit into the hypothetical photo of their fantasy weekend. I don't know if I *truly* believe it, but it has crossed my mind. Because with cocktail, it seems like you either get it or you don't, and there is absolutely no in between.

'The dress is cocktail,' my work colleague said, while handing me a paper invitation to a company social in a few weeks: one of those events that businesses put on to keep spirits high and employee-turnover costs low.

'Oh, fun!' I said and took the invitation. I had only just started this job at a company of about 350 normal people, and I had decided to take on the persona of someone who said things like, 'Oh, fun!' unironically and asked, 'How was your weekend?'

at the coffee machine. 'What are you wearing to this?' I said faux-casually to the girl who sat next to me.

'Um, I don't know,' she said while staring intently at her screen, signalling that I had now been categorised as a frivolous girl and not a serious girl, the kind of frivolous girl who plans her outfits two weeks in advance because she loves outfits so much. She probably had a closet full of outfits that were perfect for this occasion anyway. She probably had dresses that she had worn to the polo and her cousin's wedding and a couple of pieces she picked up after spotting them in the window while strolling down the street. She didn't need them for a specific occasion, they were 'just in case' purchases. 'You just never know!' she probably said afterwards to her friends (they're on the same netball team) and her mother-in-law while they drank mimosas at 2pm. Choosing a cocktail dress isn't a terrifying prospect when opening your closet is like walking out of the elevator onto the fanciest floor of David Jones.

'Yeah, I don't know either!' I said with a loud, fake horse laugh, as if she had been the one to ask the question. I didn't bring it up again. While staring at my new, fancy desktop computer, I thought about how I'd never had to worry about cocktail dresses at my old job – though at that job there had once been a morning when everyone got to work to find someone had smashed a TV through the front door. There was just shattered glass, no door and a TV sitting on the floor, and the council wouldn't remove the TV because it was on private property. It wasn't really a cocktail dress kind of place.

I ended up wearing a shapeless black linen dress (which had a mysterious white stain on it that could have been candle wax or bleach) that I wore almost once a week, trying to jazz up my look by adding eyeliner and flat black sandals that pinched my foot sides. I got it wrong.

King Edward aside, it seems most likely that the cocktail dress code was invented around the same time as the cocktail dress in the 1920s. This was a shorter version of the formal dresses of the time, one that allowed you to move around social gatherings with more ease – presumably to make covert deals about bootlegging gin. In a 1936 film called *The Ex-Mrs Bradford*, a blonde bombshell called Jean Arthur says that a cocktail dress is 'something to spill cocktails on', which I know is just a funny thing to say and is untrue, otherwise we'd all be walking around in bin-bag togas. Basically, if you're not familiar with this particular lifestyle – a lifestyle of days at the races and weekends at wineries and … ah … champagne museum galas? I don't know – your only recourse is to figure out what 'cocktail' is by figuring out what it is not. This is what I have learnt that it is *not*, from attending a handful of cocktail events in my life (three, maybe four):

- A ball gown with a train, definitely not that.
- I mean it – do not wear a ball gown! Put that ball gown back into storage (A basement full of dry ice? The weekend cottage owned by your great uncle, the Count? Paris Hilton's

closet in *The Bling Ring*, with the stripper pole and all those pillows with her face on it?).

- Pants. Unless they're made out of ... silk?
- Anything that ASOS suggests is 'cocktail appropriate'.

What I'm saying is that it must be a garment that makes you seem as playful as a gust of wind whipping up one's hem, has the power of a raging cyclone ripping up the roots of thousand-year-old trees, and gives the wearer the unmistakable sensation of being levitated from atop a tall hill, the tumultuous air gathering underneath your open umbrella and carrying you, lifting lifting lifting like Icarus towards the sun!

Basically, I don't know. Knowing if you've gotten it right often requires a lot of feedback, too. *Would this work????* you write to friends in Slack channels and Facebook group messages, sending links to items that you know can be express shipped in three days or less. *Is this okay????* you'll text to other friends once you're wearing the outfit, accompanied by a full-body photo of you making a pained face in your grubby mirror.

You look fine, your friends will always reply, which is not actually a signal that you do actually look fine, but could signal that they are exasperated with this two-week-long conversation – and with you – and you better stop right now lest you be the anecdote at their next cocktail party, which you will not be invited to.

Naturally, it's usually the most stressful events that require this delicate decoding. I might be imagining it, but the social occasions I have dreaded most have also involved a cocktail dress code. Say, weddings for people I don't really know, which involve me either hiding in the toilet for 80 per cent of the night or getting catastrophically drunk and saying things like, 'Who wants to talk about Taylor Swift and Kanye West?' to groups of people in the hope that they will challenge me. Or, industry events that I have neither the networking skills nor public profile to legitimately attend. Somehow, these are the ones that I always forget to prepare for. Have you ever attended a party where everyone was wearing suits and chandelier earrings, and you turned up in scuffed Dr Martens and with a stained white tote bag? But it's too late to do anything about it? And then you got introduced to Ronan Farrow, who had recently won a Pulitzer Prize? And you said, 'I'm dressed a bit casual!' and he looked at you like you were a baby deer who had just plopped out of the birth canal and was attempting to stand for the first time but kept slipping on birthing fluid? Well, I have, which is why I know it's important to figure out what 'cocktail' means.

Of course, the anxiety that you're not quite dressed correctly isn't reserved for adulthood. At primary school, casual clothes days were absolutely rife with landmines. *What does 'casual' mean to them?* I would think to myself, trying to subtly discern what other people (children, really) were planning on wearing without giving away the fact that I was thinking about it too much. Thinking about stuff too much is the enemy of casual clothes day. But, of course, 'casual' means such different things to different people. (Is it jeans? IS IT TRACKSUIT PANTS???)

One St Patrick's Day, I told my mum I wouldn't dress in all-green casual clothes because I didn't know for sure if my classmates would – I didn't want to seem *that* Irish. All the kids in my class were pretty much first-generation Greek or Italian or Vietnamese, and I didn't need to remind them that I wasn't. Naturally, that day everyone in the school was dressed in green casual clothes and I was dressed in my uniform, which gave me a vaguely self-hating and uniform-loving vibe that my mum found very amusing. I never again approached a casual clothes day without gathering intel first.

Getting it right means so much but it also means nothing, because here's the thing: they're just *clothes*. They're just different materials stitched together that we strategically tangle around our bodies so that our sensitive parts don't show. They're not better or worse than each other; they're not really anything. But somehow they still signal to our peers that we desire to behave correctly, are prepared to match them in a ritual, and that there is no need to panic because things are going *exactly to plan*.

Even though this is a very adolescent instinct, there is a very small part of my heart – a part that relishes getting it deliberately wrong – that I'd like to protect. Because it means they haven't quite got you yet. It means you know that it's all a farce, really, that the only code you care about is your own and you're willing to prove it.

The last cocktail event I went to before the world shut down was at the opening night of a film festival, which I wasn't nervous about because I had attended this event before. It was the sort of thing where I knew I would run into other awkward people who also never usually attend events, and we would make *oh GOD* faces to each other from across the room and clutch each other's arms like liferafts. This time, I decided that instead of borrowing an outfit that I was scared of ruining, or buying a weird dress on Afterpay that I would never wear again, it was okay to wear a pair of plain black pants – pants I had owned for many years and that had survived sitting on curbs, being splashed with beer and being worn at Meredith Music Festival. I wasn't the kind of girl who had fancy outfits that hung in her closet 'just in case'. That was okay. After work I smugly took my easily-foldable night-time outfit into the toilets to change, feeling as though I had cracked some code of unattainable, genteel femininity.

I hadn't worn the pants in a while, and when 5.30pm rolled around, I realised mid-zip-up that the reason I hadn't worn the pants in a while was because they were now a bit too tight on the tummy. It was too late to turn back, so I just lay parallel on the closed lid of the work toilet and sucked in my intestines until I could do them up, praying the plastic button wouldn't pop and trying to remember how to do a French tuck to disguise the straining fabric. There was a mark on them that several splashes from the sink couldn't remove. 'It'll be dark,' I said to no one.

A few hours later, while rummaging the artistic grazing table of stacked cheeses, mounds of meat and strategically placed bread sticks, I dropped a hunk of salami on the floor. As I leaned over to pick it up, I heard the pop of a button.

Costumes of coolness throughout history (that you can unsuccessfully copy)

Plato

When you are cool, people just believe the things that you say. I know this to be true because I have heard cool people say some truly wild things that they have not been confronted for. Once, a cool person said to me – in front of their boss – 'I'm going to have a two-hour nap in the conference room, just wake me if anything weird happens on the internet.' I've witnessed a cool girl say, 'I never remember how unattractive people can be until I go back on Tinder,' and not one unattractive person in the room (and there were a few) challenged her on this. When you're cool you can say almost anything.

Plato was cool and he knew this, which is why he invented universities – so people could be more like him. Aristotle tried to be like him, but wasn't like him enough to be the big boss of Plato's university when Plato died. This is a hard but common lesson for those associated with cool people: coolness is not always transferrable. Whenever you see sculptures and paintings of Plato, he has this dense triangular beard that looks like folds of soft clouds tumbling out of his face and he is wearing a very flowy, layered tunic. He also always looks furious. Sometimes in these pictures of his likeness he doesn't even have eyeballs, as if he is so mad at you for not understanding his theory of forms that his eyes have literally disintegrated inside his skull. Maybe everyone in Greece in the 380s was wearing identical tunics, but there's something about how mad Plato looks at all times that makes his tunic cooler.

(Just as an aside, once, I found myself at a party with a multicoloured light-up dancefloor – which is unusual, as I'm not usually invited to parties that put that much thought into the aesthetics of the ground – when I heard a cool girl shout at me over the noise of music and people: 'What's your favourite scholar?' she said. 'Haha, weird!' I said. 'I guess, Plato?' She looked at me blankly. 'What's your favourite *colour*?' she repeated. I faked a laugh. She looked down at the colourful floor and danced away.)

Patti Smith

Patti Smith is so cool that if you ever attempted to wear clothes like her or cut your hair to look like hers, everyone around you would immediately assume that you've had some sort of mental breakdown and intend to adopt the public persona of 'lunatic'. But Patti Smith never looks like a lunatic. Patti Smith is so cool that one afternoon she decided, *Hey, I want to have hair like Keith Richards,* and so just cut her own hair with a pair of blunt scissors and ended up looking cooler than Keith Richards has ever looked in his life.

Patti Smith's coolness is not an alienating coolness, but still can't be replicated by people who are not cool. Salvador Dalí once called her a 'gothic crow', which is possibly the nicest and most sincere thing that a surrealist is capable of saying. In the '70s, she would go to a Salvation Army store, buy a bunch of white men's shirts, some black slacks and the kind of faded blazer that looks like it has endured the ash of a million cigarettes, put them on and look better than anyone who had ever lived. Then she would grab a tin of anchovies, put them in a roll and eat it while writing poetry all night at the Chelsea Hotel. Even if you did complete that sequence of casually chic activities, no one would believe you.

Hunter S Thompson

Just putting on a terry-towelling bucket hat and a Hawaiian shirt does not make you cool. Take off the aviators. Please return that cigarette holder. Your articles don't always need to involve you experiencing the more banal aspects of the world while under the influence of amphetamines. You're embarrassing us all.

James Spader

If you hate James Spader, it could be because you find him so cool that it makes you uneasy in the part of your soul that likes it when someone says something mean and funny about the friend who you find annoying sometimes. We're speaking specifically, of course, about 1980s-era James Spader, and even more specifically about *Pretty in Pink*-era James Spader. In this movie he plays Steff, a rich teenage asshole who is also the human equivalent of a line of cocaine. Steff is very cool.

Steff wears linen suits to school, which are sometimes entirely white. Steff looks more sophisticated on an average day at school than most people look at their weddings. He often has a cigarette hanging out of his mouth, in that dangly way cool people master that suggests the universe has afforded them so much good fortune that they can successfully defy the laws of gravity. James Spader's hair during this time looks artfully ruffled, like it has just caught the wind and somehow been frozen that way.

Steff says stuff like, 'If we're gonna shoot, we've got to shake it,' because when you're cool you don't have to make any sense or ever explain yourself (he also spits on the floor of the school corridor like it's grass, and his teachers don't even bat an eyelid). His voice suggests that he is bored of everything and you will never be capable of holding his attention for more than a few seconds, unless you are a dangling cigarette. Steff is a dick but sometimes people who are dicks are cool and, frankly, we all have to live with that.

Jean-Michel Basquiat

Jean-Michel Basquiat was too busy creating cultural movements to follow any subculture's dress code, and was so cool that talking about his clothes feels absurd. He was so cool that Blondie asked him to play a DJ in their video for 'Rapture'. He looked cooler as a fake DJ than the real band did, which was inevitable. Everyone wanted to be near him because he made everyone else seem like tame has-beens, which is a deeply uncomfortable and exciting feeling to have.

When he posed in photos with Andy Warhol – which he did often – he always looked more dynamic and cutting-edge, even if he and Andy Warhol wore exactly the same thing. It wasn't what Jean-Michel wore, but *how*: a certain button left unbuttoned, a skivvy poking out from beneath a baggy black jumper, a flannelette shirt that looked like it had been washed with rocks and bleach on top of a grey polo top that looked like it cost $3999. Every photo of Jean-Michel Basquiat and Andy Warhol should be captioned *Jean-Michel and a fan*.

Marie Antoinette

I have made some enemies in my life (two, maybe three), but none have actively hated me enough to attempt to slice my head clean from my body, which tells me that I don't have a cool enough personality to inspire this kind of passion. Marie Antoinette did. People hated her so much that they could not get enough of her, which I guess makes her a bit like Kim Kardashian, but maybe more like eating a tasty dessert that you know will give you diarrhoea later.

In the 1770s they didn't have Twitter, so when people decided that they hated you they would send around pamphlets saying that you were probably an Austrian spy, were likely setting up a lesbian orgy syndicate in Versailles and maybe even ate babies – who's to say? But before the Third Estate considered Marie Antoinette a gross symbol of aristocratic excess, they were very much 'oooh, cool dress'. Marie Antoinette was an influencer in the sense that she actually influenced fashion, not in the sponsored-content-laxative-tea way.

Part of her coolness was that you just didn't have enough money to dress like her. Can't afford a silk gown trimmed with fur, ribbon and actual jewels? Embarrassing! Don't have a metre-tall powdered wig with feathers of extinct birds jutting out the top? Sorry! Marie Antoinette's dresses were so wild that her mum, Maria, even wrote to her once saying, *You need to cool it with the dresses, also are you really having all those orgies, y/n?* You know you are cool when everyone hates you, even your mum.

Harold Perrineau

Harold Perrineau played Michael in *Lost*, but that's not as important as when he played Mercutio in Baz Luhrmann's

Romeo + Juliet. Harold Perrineau is the most important person in *Romeo + Juliet*. Evidence: the most important scenes in the film are, a) when Mercutio wears a sequined halter top and performs 'Young Hearts Run Free' at the Capulets' party, and b) when he dies, while wearing a crucifix necklace and a sheer white shirt that he has forgotten to do up. It may not even have buttons. If Romeo did that, he would look like a dickhead.

The only person in that movie who comes close to Harold Perrineau's level of coolness is John Leguizamo playing Tybalt. Tybalt wears tight suits and a bulletproof vest with a picture of Jesus Christ on it. Guns aren't cool, but if they were cool it would be John Leguizamo's fault.

Ned Kelly

Imagine anyone else putting a metal bucket on their head and still looking cool; Ned Kelly was the coolest person to ever exist in Australia.

Joan Didion

Joan Didion is a terrifying cool person. It feels like if you ever met Joan Didion, she would look at you through her oversized sunglasses – but not at your body, at your *soul* – take a drag of her cigarette and say something withering that would ruin your entire life. She wouldn't even remember what she had said to you, that's how inconsequential the interaction would be to her. Unless you're a baby wandering around Haight-Ashbury on LSD, you're probably not worth her time. In photographs, she often has an expression that suggests she has just said, '… and?'

When you think about California in the 1960s, you don't usually think of long-sleeved shirts and thick turtlenecks, but Joan Didion is so cool that this seemed like the only acceptable uniform for a glamorous writer. You can imagine her wrapped in layers of cashmere no matter the outside temperature, because when you're that incisive your blood turns to ice in your veins. Her cardigans would be the softest cardigans you have ever felt in your life, and would make everything that you touch thereafter feel like lava. Maybe she's cold all the time because she drinks Coca-Cola for breakfast and eats salted almonds for lunch, but even this seems like an extremely cool and unsafe way to live your life.

Rihanna

Don't even try.

In my cart

In my cart, right now, is the recipe for my happiness.

As I am adding clothes to my cart – yep, get in there! You too! – I am an active participant in my own wellbeing and am identifying the building blocks I need to construct a wonderful castle of contentment for myself, a castle where I am secure and very happy. When I own the things in this cart, everything I will ever need will be at my fingertips, as if I was standing in a kitchen in a Nancy Meyers movie. Like, emotionally. Dopamine toasts my blood like a warm bath and a generous pour of a buttery chardonnay.

I am creating a small family in this cart! This goes with that thing! These two items are siblings! Oh, the places I'll go in these two things! Oh, how perfect I will look and feel! A whole bloodline, an ecosystem is being created in this tiny, wonderful universe that is actually just a cart! They have hopes and dreams, they live and breathe, they have tiny heartbeats inside this cart!

Isn't it funny that it's just a *click* and it's done? *Click*! It is as easy as that! Isn't it miraculous? One click and I will feel unparalleled bliss, bliss that must resemble the humbling tranquillity you feel when looking at the Niagara Falls or the Great Barrier Reef, or how those Hawaiians felt when they killed Captain Cook.

In this cart there is redemption, there is wisdom, there is acceptance, there is forgiveness, there is a floral boob tube I saw on Instagram on a girl I sort of know; she works in fashion and always seems to be at these daytime dance parties where everyone is drinking orange drinks and dressed in linen.

The combination of items in this cart – a good cart, a diverse cart – feels like a kaleidoscope of all my aesthetic tastes, an exciting mix of high and low, the most pure distillation of the creative potential of my mind. I am a genius.

Am I a stylist?

Okay, I know I am not a stylist, but the time I have spent scrolling through the endless pages on this website (how long has it been? It wasn't dark when I started …) and finding these pieces, which are often hidden in rows of less-nice pieces, suggests that I have a good eye and discerning taste that is *unusual* for a non-stylist. That's all I'm saying.

Okay, now that I have realised I've been operating in US dollars and not Australian dollars this whole time, I have a little more perspective, i.e. these carefree and quirky socks are now $50 and I actually don't think I am living that life right now. Still a very good cart, though!

Why do I have two different shapeless black sack dresses in this cart? I'm always buying shapeless black sack dresses. I have a wardrobe full of identical black sack dresses. Am I an Italian widow in the 1950s? Why do I dress like a pre-Vatican II nun?

I am not going to wear this floral boob tube, am I? I don't go to dance parties during the day. I don't order the orange drinks because I always drink them too quickly, and they're always like $14, and then I end up drinking seven of them and have Too Many Opinions.

I have some invoices being paid next week, hopefully.

Oh my god, what is that shipping? Why is the shipping *so* expensive? Just for my humble cart? My tiny, little cart? My insignificant cart of cheap materials folded tightly? How are they *shipping* it?? Is it a package tied to a single drone? Is it just one man in a paddle boat? Is it like one of those transport systems in *Star Trek* where you can put a thing in one end and then the molecules just remake themselves on the other end?

Oh, it's timed out.

The Coven

A long time ago, certainly before you were born, if a woman in your social circle annoyed you, you could accuse her of being a witch and that would be the end of it. They would take her away, make her say the Lord's Prayer, poke her and prod her, squish her between two rocks, tie her up and chuck her in a lake. If she somehow survived all of this, then she was a witch. In any case, you likely would not see her at brunch the next day*.

Whether it's due to Tumblr or *The Craft*, at some point being a witch was presented as the thing you *want* to be and not the person you wanted to get rid of. It meant that you belonged and were privy to secrets that others were not privy to. (Especially men, but it's not difficult to keep secrets from men. They're very easily distracted and, frankly, I do not know how they have survived thus far.) Light a candle, grow your hair long, chuck on some

---

* This also describes the behaviour of any group of white women on a reality show, starting with Laguna Beach in 2004.

50

Lana Del Rey and voila! You're suddenly part of a community, a member of a movement that is bigger than yourself, and without any threat of pitchfork-wielding townspeople tying you to the rack for identifying with the wrong subculture.

I have never seen the rack or any kind of instrument of torture in real life, but I guess the closest thing I have encountered is a reformer Pilates machine, which I assume is designed to give you a flat stomach and a firm butt and is not intentionally designed to dislocate each of your joints one by one. Yet this does cross my mind every time I lie down on one. I once saw a woman slip off a reformer and ricochet off a wall. I once saw a woman topple off the wooden platform and get dragged down by one of the straps that was meant to be strengthening her biceps. I have fallen off reformers more times than I can count. During a reformer Pilates class, I would confess to almost anything.

I started doing reformer Pilates a few years ago, because my workmates Tess and Mel wanted to do it. They were both fit, and I knew that being fit was something that I needed to be, so once a week, on our lunch breaks, we would walk to a nearby Pilates studio in the city to take the Level 1 class run by a woman named Heidi.

Heidi had the calm, measured and somewhat menacing demeanour that I would expect from someone who had access to nuclear codes or who was secretly a murderous robot. I never saw her with a full frown, but I never saw her with a full grin either – her mouth was perpetually frozen in this serene smile, like a benevolent cult leader on a propaganda poster. Despite the Level 1 designation on the class timetable, I have never been in more physical pain than what Heidi put me through. 'I hate Heidi,' my work friends and I would say to each other as we limped back to the office, or tried to stand up from our chairs, or leaned down to plug in our laptops. Although we hated Heidi, we loved talking about how much we hated her, because it was a way we could remind ourselves that we had attended Pilates.

Sometimes Heidi had to go back to the factory to be re-wired, so we would have replacement teachers who varied in sadism. A tiny woman named Laz had obvious favourites in the class, which were the women who were good at Pilates. 'You're all killing it today!' she announced one day, walking quickly between the machines as we wove long wooden poles around our legs for reasons of fitness. At that exact moment, I dropped my pole with a big *clang*. 'Well, you *were* all killing it!' Laz said, with a laugh. A few of her favourites laughed. I wondered if I should kill Laz after class.

I liked another teacher, Jenny, slightly more, because she sometimes made references that made me think that she watched TV, which meant that there had to be at least fifteen minutes in the day when she was doing something that was bad for her. Once, when someone in class sneezed and another person said, 'God bless you – I better say it if no one else will!' Jenny started laughing.

'Isn't that from *Seinfeld?*' Jenny said.

'Yes, haha,' the other woman said.

'Thank goodness there's another *Seinfeld* fan in here,' Jenny said warmly.

The rest of the class was silent. Everyone who had not laughed at the reference was now rendered a cultural Luddite. We'd probably never even seen an episode of *Seinfeld*.

I know Seinfeld *VERY well, actually, I'm just too busy trying to remain vertical over here to perform it,* I thought angrily.

'Yeah, a guy at work likes *Seinfeld*, haha,' said the girl. Jenny's smile slipped slightly, and she walked to another reformer.

It didn't really matter who the teacher was – every class still felt like torture. It didn't help when they said the challenge was 'all mental', because even when I went in with a mentally strong attitude (*I Am A Powerful Woman, I Will Not Spew*, etc.) I still ended up the worst one in the class, making Lucille Ball faces while trying to lift a leg that didn't quite go diagonal for whatever reason. Wasn't my body capable? Wasn't it built to withstand hardship and protect young and be connected to the waning of the moon and to sync with every living organism in the frenetic cosmos? And if it wasn't, if I laid really still on the machine, could I convince them that I was actually dead? And in the time it would take them all to confer with each other about me being dead ('Do corpses sweat that much? Wow.') class time would be up and I could just walk out of there?

I don't engage in that kind of self-talk, I'd tell myself whenever I drifted off into these fantasies of rendering myself so limp and passive that I would be carried out of the class by paramedics. 'I am a feminist.'

Tess and I eventually got to a point where we *needed* to go to Pilates at lunch on Tuesday no matter what else was happening, because it would somehow mean something if we didn't. We were Pilates Women now. We may not have been the same as the chic yo-pros who rocked up fifteen minutes early in their matching two-piece workout clothes; who knew all the moves; who didn't even need to slurp water during class; whose hair was tied up in elegant ponytails; who were probably executives in board rooms; who probably CC-ed and BCC-ed their colleagues depending on the situation, but we were at least adjacent to them. I was obsessed with these women.

One day, our regular class was booked up, so Tess booked us into the sister studio a few blocks away. 'It's a different class, but I'm sure it'll be fine,' she said between puffs as we ran from our office to the studio. We arrived just in time, already sweating, and immediately realised that this place was … different. This was the CEO Pilates studio. There were four different types of tea available in the waiting room. There were cubicles in the changing room. The receptionist asked us, 'How *are* you?' with such careful intensity that I wondered if she was actually a psychologist who they'd booked to work reception. Tess and I quickly changed into baggy, faded slogan T-shirts and forced stiff leggings onto our hot, rubbery legs.

'This is the Level 2 class,' I said to Tess, pointing to the sign on the door. We had never done Level 2 before. I couldn't even conceive that a class could be harder than the one we usually took. Would they expect us to levitate?

'Should be fine!' said Tess, who hated admitting she couldn't do things.

It was immediately a disaster. Even the warm-up was impossible. We were surrounded by heavenly creatures – women of all sizes and shapes, colours and ages – who were able to contort their bodies into beautiful letters of the alphabet. They could hold two weighted balls while standing on one leg and pushing the carriage with another. They suspended themselves with one hand. Their cores seemed to have the strength of tractors.

We knew we had made a mistake. I kept shooting Tess mean sidelong glances like she had abandoned me in the trenches of Normandy or encouraged me to go blonde. After a while we were making so many huffing and puffing noises, and then disbelieving laughing noises, that the heavenly creatures started glancing at us in disdain. We were disturbing their practise. We had polluted their heaven.

'Okay, girls,' said the teacher, not bothering to hide her annoyance at the two non-desirables who had poisoned her tranquil space.

'I feel like we connected on a whole new level that day,' Tess told me recently when we were recalling that horrible afternoon. Not long after that we both abandoned the class. We had quit our jobs, and without Tess egging me on, I didn't have the motivation for such a strenuous lunchtime activity and so went back to reading and not talking to anyone. Despite her perilous can-do attitude, Tess had lost the taste for reformer Pilates as well. We had tried to belong, but it hadn't stuck. We had chosen the wrong coven. Perhaps we weren't even witches. 'That class was more difficult than childbirth,' said Tess, who had actually recently given birth to her first child. 'At least childbirth has breaks.'

It wasn't until later that I realised how much that 'can my body physically do this?' energy had affected my outlook on the whole saga. Is it possible that the teachers were right? Did I – like every protagonist in every sports movie ever – have a mental barrier I needed to break through? As a way to keep in touch now that we weren't working together, Tess and I would sometimes do nature walks on the weekend. Tess was a seasoned hiker – multi-day in Peru sort of seasoned – and one day suggested we do a mini hike to see if I could do it. She packed me a trail mix with mini M&Ms in it and told me exactly how much water to bring. It was a hot day, and I felt unsure if I could trust my body to walk up inclines and balance on rocks, but after a forty-minute drive in which we listened to the entirety of Lorde's *Melodrama*, we set off.

'This is taking a bit longer than usual,' said Tess, confused, after we had been walking for a couple of hours. It turned out we had accidentally taken the 10-kilometre route instead of the 2-kilometre one, and it was too late to turn back now. We laughed so much at this mistake that we needed to stop walking so we could breathe properly. But laughing didn't seem to be a problem in this club. Old couples nodded to us as they walked past.

'Nice day!' said a man in spandex who was sweating profusely.

'Yeah!' I said, and I meant it.

When we reached the end of the trail, aching and covered in dirt, our bellies full of mini M&Ms, I felt strangely emotional. I wasn't used to actually completing a physical activity; I usually found a way to stop or cut it short and generally wimp out much earlier than that. I had done the whole thing. My legs had worked the way I'd always heard they could. I went home and cradled my knees to my chest and felt something like pride.

I recently started going to reformer Pilates again, at a small studio near my new office. I've got a teacher named Sarah who laughs at herself when she tells us to 'push harder!' and apologises when she instructs us to do something that hurts. 'Good work!' she barks at me after every class, even when I have done very bad work. We both know it's not true, but sometimes you need to lie to keep things moving along. Witches are good like that.

The mind

'A leopard can't change its spots, but an annoying person can change their personality. Maybe!'

—*Jeremiah, 13:23*

Narc energy

It began with the storms, which stretched London's structural integrity to such a point that a city's worth of shit and piss from the sewers started pouring into the swollen Thames. London being a place where, historically, shit and piss has run along gutters like brown, fecal veins of the city, this was not particularly remarkable, but what *was* notable was that this time the sewers were also overflowing with cocaine.

A team from King's College London determined that the levels of cocaine detected in the Thames was much higher than could be detected in any other river. A few years earlier, a study by the European Monitoring Centre for Drugs and Drug Addiction had found that, in fact, London had the highest concentration of cocaine in its sewage of any city in Europe. You might not have a globe in front of you right now, but know that there really are a lot of cities in Europe. Cities full of law firms, and modelling agencies, and superclubs that you'll never see because you won't make it past the leather-clad doorman. People in London love cocaine, we must assume; people in London love to go to a pub, drink warm beer, talk about Margaret Thatcher, get a bit sleepy, take some cocaine, get worked up about Brexit or *(What's the Story) Morning Glory?*, wee out the cocaine, and then get pushed into the street to participate in a soccer brawl. The rest of the things may not be true, but it seems that the first thing is certainly true.

The main problem with London's previously innocent rivers becoming cocaine rivers was, of course, the eels. What would happen to the eels in the rivers, eels that were already endangered? (You can tell they know that, too: in photos, eels always look like you've just caught them screaming in panic.) How would the cocaine urine affect them? Would they stay up all day and all night? Would they continue to ask each other enthusiastic rhetorical questions? Would they race around to various non-existent engagements while feeling quite, quite warm?

If I have anything in common with an eel (I can't swim, but I don't presume to know everything that happens in an eel's day) it's that there's reason to believe drugs won't necessarily make me any more fun to hang out with. 'You don't seem like someone who has ever taken drugs,' a girl at work recently told me, and I said, 'Thanks!' and then wondered if I should be thanking her. You know how in movies and at first-year uni parties there's always one tall guy in loose pants who asks, 'Do you party?' with a smug smile as a way to ascertain if someone binge drinks and is opening to drug-taking? As if there is only one correct way to party, and without those ways you're not technically or spiritually at a party? This I imagine is the conundrum for the eels, who didn't have a choice as to whether they were going to take cocaine or not, but if they *did* have the choice, perhaps would be disappointed by the actual experience as compared to the cultural cachet of the experience.

Some Italian biologists at the University of Naples Federico II were concerned about the eels. It is unclear why they were unconcerned about the other marine wildlife in the Thames; perhaps they had encountered eels on cocaine before and knew that they were one species that shouldn't be trusted on the gear. They put some eels in tanks and then spiked the water with the same amount of cocaine that they thought was in the Thames. They did this for fifty days, which is a long time for *anyone* to take cocaine, let alone an eel (just a normal eel, not even an eel who works in advertising).

Eventually the Italian biologists concluded that, just like a human who's taken low levels of cocaine for fifty days, the eels seemed noticeably more hyperactive than usual. What was more concerning was that even when the eels had been in rehab for ten days (imagine *28 Days*, but Sandra Bullock is an eel), the cocaine stayed in their gills and other tissues and changed the way their hormones carried messages. 'It is likely that in this condition, the reproduction of the eels could be impaired,' Anna Capaldo, the lead author of the study, told *National Geographic* – presumably after being asked, 'The eels can still fuck, though, right?'

The evidence was conclusive: eels really shouldn't be taking cocaine. Some English researchers suggested that the Italian biologists had used more cocaine than is actually in the Thames, but the general message was the same. Sure, cocaine might help you swim to the Sargasso Sea quicker, but you won't be able to make love to the other eels once you get there.

It has always irked me when people brag about taking drugs. (For reference: I am talking about party drugs from a very privileged, insufferable, middle-class point of view, as if that viewpoint wasn't already obvious.) This is partly because I don't understand why people brag about taking them when *it is so easy to buy and consume drugs*. It's one of the easiest things you can do! It's like showing off about watching a movie you downloaded or eating a sandwich that was handed to you by your mum. Experimenting with MDMA in Berlin is not as impressive as you think it is, Carla!

The first time I (knowingly) saw a girl my age who was high was at the party of some older guys I had met during high school. She was walking down a corridor and then walked directly into a wall, as if she thought it would melt away as soon as she reached it. She fell like a plank onto the ground, then picked herself up and started walking, Pac Man-style, down a different corridor as if nothing had happened. I did too many embarrassing things when I was sober to risk inhaling.

If party drugs were an essential component to particular cool situations (like when people say that you don't understand certain EDM until you've taken ecstasy, which shouldn't be true but maybe is) then there were certain echelons of coolness and acceptance that couldn't be reached unless you tried them. As a teenager, I was told to watch *24 Hour Party People* so I could understand what it was 'really' like, but concluded that of course taking drugs would have been good while you were watching fucking New Order in 1980. Like everything else, it seemed like taking drugs would never be as good as it had been in the past, at the birthplace of musical movements and the nucleus of culture. It had to happen in large warehouses that were pitch-black except for brilliant, flashing pink and blue lights; places that swarmed like a disturbed anthill with quick-moving bodies; where sweat dripped on the walls, mysterious materials crunched and stuck underfoot, and 'Blue Monday' was pulsing in the background. Missing out on formative social scenarios and seeming uptight felt like a bad option, but the other option wasn't fail-safe either. Sure it looked fun and some people didn't act any differently, but for others it seemed like drugs opened the floodgates for already obnoxious people to act even more obnoxious: to be a little louder, hug strangers more and take people's heads in their hands while saying something about their eyeballs that made no sense. What if that obnoxious person was *me*?

If London is the place where eels find cocaine to be readily available, then the same must be said for Australians visiting New York. I knew a lot of people who had visited New York for a few weeks, taken a lot of drugs, then come back and discussed that time they took a lot of drugs in New York for several years after. These stories always involved the traveller ending up somewhere weird: a private party at an art gallery, a minor celebrity's house, a karaoke party of only Dolly Parton songs.

For example, you meet a friend of a friend who works at a store that sells Australian goods such as ugg boots and eucalyptus hand cream. She's not Australian, but that doesn't seem to matter. She somehow knows a lot of rich and interesting people; sometimes they're only interesting because they're rich. You follow her to art openings and rooftop parties and taco trucks. Once, in a stranger's basement apartment, when it is silently determined that despite your obvious narc energy you are not judgemental about people taking drugs, you are pulled by the friend of a friend into a bathroom with her giggling girlfriend. 'I know what you're doing!' someone calls, laughing. Your boyfriend and you exchange a look as you're dragged into the bathroom for your initiation into this mysterious female coven of acceptance. The doe-eyed girl towers over you, shoves a finger into a snap-lock bag for sandwiches then sticks a dirty, eucalyptus-scented fingernail up your nose. It happens so quickly that you don't have time to be alarmed. She isn't watching you carefully, and you wonder if you should sneeze some on the floor. You spend the rest of the night making up dance routines in the mirror of a ballet studio that is inexplicably in the building's basement. You find out later from your boyfriend that the girl is known to take a lot of cocaine, but you wonder if this assessment has more to do with the fact that she is thin, full of energy and never has much interest in food, a quality that he is absolutely baffled by.

There's a line from a 50 Cent song that I used to sing along to when I was fourteen, in which he tells the woman he's with that he has some ecstasy, 'if you into taking drugs'. It always struck me as such a low-pressure way to convey that: doesn't matter if you do, doesn't matter if you don't. It's just for your own personal enjoyment, after all. You know, if you *feel* like it, it's here. Nothing to do with dirty bathrooms or social situations that feel akin to watching a puppy hang their head out the window of a moving car and being worried that one sudden movement from the car will see that curious puppy go tumbling out. (I saw that happen to a puppy once – and it lived! That hasn't stopped me thinking of the possibility of that same puppy not living almost every day since.) Maybe you would have a transcendent and lovely moment in your own body, leaping into the dark with your friends, your heart feeling like it might burst for the gratitude you have for the universe – or you could be having a weird time listening to music in a country field and then bump into your boss, freak out and say, 'Ah, I have to go to an appointment!' and then run off into the night. You know, for example.

Part of getting older is reaching the unfortunate conclusion that alcohol and other drugs have the power to make you magically more free-spirited, interesting and easygoing for a night, then the next day often leave you feeling like your entire brain is coated in cement and your entire life is coated in misery. I put a lot of obvious effort into appearing carefree, without considering that I was exhausting myself with the consuming performance of seeming relaxed. This is not a conversation you want to have with people who are sober *or* who are high: the former will quickly realise that you're likely to be the 'freak out' kind of party partner instead of the 'notice funny things about the sky' party partner; the latter will look at you blankly and then walk into a dark forest just to escape the self-conscious chaos of your mind.

Some people take drugs to induce a temporary absence of shame, because not feeling shame is the most punk thing you can do, really. I wonder if eels ever feel ashamed. I wonder if eels ever feel self-conscious about anything. I wonder if when they were swimming around the Thames, high, they felt like they had purpose, resolve, confidence. When I looked to see if anything else had happened to the eels, I found an article on the *Independent* website with the headline: *Record cocaine levels in Thames probably not making fish high, experts say.*

A man named James Robson, who is a senior curator at the SEA LIFE London Aquarium, said that the eels probably wouldn't be ingesting as much cocaine as the Italians suggested and that the situation was not as dire as first thought. 'You haven't got a lot of disco-dancing fish down the bottom of the Thames,' he said. He suggested that we should all be a bit more concerned about climate change killing the eels than cocaine.

And wet wipes. 'Anyone hoping to do their bit to protect the river should consider stopping using wet wipes,' the article soberly concluded. What a comedown.

Anna-Grace

You believe that you're beyond it, but you're probably not. You might say that you never even think about it – you're too occupied with things that actually matter. You're busy thinking about being kind to others, or using canvas bags over plastic bags, or researching the candidates before you vote in local council elections, or decreasing your screen time, or buying from small businesses instead of giant corporate online emporiums, or stopping yourself from murdering your enemies and throwing their remains in the sea. You know, good human-being stuff.

But I think you also care about seeming uncool. I'm sorry to be the one to tell you, but it's true. It may not play on your mind as much as the, *Is the world ending?* thoughts, but I'm betting it occurs to you. It's not about *seeming* cool exactly, which is something that only a few people can pull off (Gertrude Stein, Jordan Catalano from *My So-Called Life*, Michelle Obama, Ian MacKaye, Prince, Sandra Oh, The Fonz etc.). It's also not about being *anti*-cool, which is subversive and, therefore, cool. It's about wanting to avoid the absence of coolness. Coolness is fragile, and even those who possess it can lose it once they get too concerned about holding onto it. Once this happens it's like *bloop!* and the bubble around them pops and suddenly their body is engulfed by fluorescent-green 'normal' air and their life as they know it is over. That's how Pablo Picasso died.

It may seem obvious, but I readily admit that I lack the self-assurance innate to cool people. I have never felt cool. It's not because I don't subscribe to conventional trends – now that would be cool. One of those live-in-the-woods, never-cut-my-hair, start-my-own-terrifying-religion, wear-a-suit-made-of-the-unrealised-curses-on-my-enemies broads. I'm not that. I take coolness very, very seriously. I have craved it, badly. If you must know, I've been studying cool people my whole life.

I was never allowed to refer to my parents as 'Mum' and 'Dad', something that I put down to being Irish without any real indication that it was. The excuse of cultural custom was a flimsy way to justify the rather embarrassing fact that I did – and still do, to be honest – call them 'Mama' and 'Dada'. (That's except for the times when I was furious at them and called them by their first names, like I was seriously considering emancipating myself from them on the spot. They never noticed.)

The older I got, the more I would avoid calling them anything when we were in other people's company, feeling like this linguistic signal betrayed every embarrassing, infantile thing about me: I got homesick on sleepovers, and played with Barbies for way too long. I didn't want to go swimming on the weekends, because I only wanted to watch *M*A*S*H* and read fictionalised accounts of World War II. When my cousins wanted to watch *Jurassic Park*, I hid in my grandfather's study after the first five minutes because I couldn't stop thinking about that cow who mooed with terror when confronted with a T-rex. I didn't care enough to stop eating cows.

This is to say that I wasn't a child who was overflowing with natural confidence. My internal compass was forever pointing at other people to tell me the right thing to be doing at any given moment. When I was almost five, my family was visiting some friends who had a three-year-old daughter called Penny. Penny, in some developmental blip, had recently cut her own hair in jagged slices across her head. The parents had laughed about it; Penny was now ridiculous.

'Haha,' I also said, probably.

When we got home, I waited until my mum started cooking dinner, went into the bathroom, and then stared at myself maniacally in the mirror while cutting a curly chunk out of my fringe.

'Oh, *Sinéad*,' my mum said in annoyance when she ran to the bathroom at the sound of dropped scissors. I don't know if she was disappointed because I had copied the actions of a child – a child who was not at all my peer and who was technically a toddler –

or because I now resembled a particularly simple-looking *Peanuts* character who she didn't want to be seen in public with.

By the time I got to primary school, it became apparent that the person I needed to be copying was a girl named Anna-Grace. This name is probably familiar to you because I mentioned her in the introduction, so if you missed that section (you were making eyes at someone on the tram/you were having a particularly violent bowel movement) it doesn't matter because I'm going to tell you about her now.

Anna-Grace had shown a VHS of *Independence Day* at her birthday party. In 1998 she was one of the first girls in our class to wear grey pants instead of grey pinafores when Christ Our Holy Redeemer Primary School bravely decided that girls wearing pants wasn't an affront. She determined the rules of all of our games (she chose who would play which Spice Girl, and only she was allowed to like Taylor Hanson). Her mum came from the Seychelles, which to me sounded like a dominion of mermaids. She never seemed stumped by a mean comment from a boy and had a knack for embarrassing them whenever they teased her, which they rarely did. We all followed her like lost ducklings who had confused an elegant swan for our mother. By the end of Grade Six she was the tallest person in the year, as if biology was trying to remind us that she was a superior specimen unbound by gravity. Anna-Grace was cool.

It's important to note that Anna-Grace wasn't exactly my *friend*. Were we friendly? Sure we were, in the same way that you're friendly with anyone who has the power to ruin your life. Let's just say that I wasn't out there borrowing Anna-Grace's scrunchie or going over to her house to watch *The Fresh Prince of Bel-Air*. I treated her with the same kind of respectful and deferential conduct you might show a town elder, or Jesus Christ.

I knew back then that I lacked coolness, which means that by the age of ten a person can know whether they have it or not. I somehow didn't know how to ride a bike or read an analogue clock, but *I knew what coolness was*. To be cool at that age you needed to be daring (saying rude words) but not reckless (saying these words in front of the teacher). You had to be aesthetically notable (wearing sneakers that lit up when you walked) but not *too* notable (wearing these sneakers before anyone had seen them advertised on Saturday morning TV). You had to be screamingly, unavoidably *normal*.

When primary school was ending I was faced with an identity crisis. Anna-Grace was going to a different high school than I was, which naturally rendered her school a far more dynamic institution than the clown college I would be attending*. I had lost my compass.

'*Why* do I have to go there, though?' I whined to my mum as she attempted to hem my new school dress, which she assured me I would 'grow into', not knowing that I would remain chain-smoking-Olsen-twin height for the rest of my life.

---

* My high school turned out to be a social-justice machine that had a gay woman as principal. It worked out okay.

'Because we like it better,' said my mum dismissively, adjusting the shoulder pads on the heavy tent of my second-hand blazer.

Naturally, at my all-girls Catholic school there were many potential Anna-Graces vying for the alpha role in the year level – loud and worldly girls who hiked their skirts up at the train station, who wore trendy T-bar sandals instead of clunky, sensible school shoes, and who made out with each other in spa baths.

It may come as no surprise when I say that this was a standard I could not replicate. I didn't have a boyfriend, and even if the prospect hadn't filled me with icy terror, I wouldn't have known how to lure one. (Stand outside the neighbouring high school with a free iPod Classic and a Hungry Jack's Whopper tied around my neck?) I wasn't allowed to go to shopping centres to just 'hang out'. I was too scared to watch scary movies, which were the most popular movies at the time, so I couldn't talk about them at school (I managed to piece together the plots of both *The Ring* and *The Others* just from overheard conversations, though). I didn't know about foundation or how to construct a messy bun that would perch artfully on the top of my head. (For those who understand the stakes of the elusive 'private-school girl hair', from 2001 to 2003 I was strictly a low-ponytail girl – that's how desperate the situation was.)

Little by little, as if I was realising that I couldn't ever be as beautiful or experienced as I needed to be to succeed, the example set by these girls started to seem less desirable. For the first time, I even started to doubt the taste of the cool people I was meant to be following – was *The Notebook* really that good? Were those *American Pie* movies actually funny? Don't all Avril Lavigne songs sound the same, though? Why would you play netball on a Saturday morning when you could lie on your bed, stare at the ceiling and contemplate the lyrics of every song on *The Eminem Show*?

To say I started consciously searching for a new identity is too neat, and it wasn't like I rocked up to school one morning with a face tattoo. But while it probably wasn't obvious to my classmates, a change was taking place in my heart. I began to seek out music that wasn't on mainstream radio, watch old movies that had won awards and read famous books that were mentioned in those movies. 'This has all been here this whole time?' I thought to myself, finding genuine joy in my discoveries and, inadvertently, some new role models. My idea of what was cool started to shift.

I stopped looking in my high-school corridor for idols. My compass was now pointing at the musicians on the cover of *NME* and the movie stars I saw in the 'Indie' section of DeeJay's Video Oakleigh. When *Almost Famous* came out on DVD, I watched it on repeat, deciding that being a music critic was the only viable career option. It didn't matter that I'd been born in 1989 and was only required to have a provable knowledge of Bloc Party, M.I.A. and *Arrested Development*, I still told anyone who would listen that *Twin Peaks* was my favourite show of all time and studiously listened to Nirvana and Smashing

Pumpkins and Red Hot Chili Peppers and Blur and Oasis and any other band that could conceivably have been on the cover of American *Rolling Stone* in the years 1991 to 1998. I worshipped a canon set by older men, the toxic air of the patriarchy filling my lungs and making me believe that, as a teenage girl, I needed to be taught what to like because my natural tastes couldn't be trusted. (This also led me to deny liking things that I thought were too 'mainstream' – some kids hid booze or porn under their bed, I hid the single of 'What's Luv?' by Fat Joe feat. Ja Rule and Ashanti.)

There were select moments when I was told I was cool, but only in relation to much more uncool things. During schoolies, a skater who dressed like he was poor but who lived in Brighton told me that I wasn't 'fake like the other girls'. I was thrilled. I had dedicated my entire adolescence to not being fake (like the other girls) and was in the process of creating an entirely fabricated identity for myself in order to achieve it. I consumed pop culture like an eager student, building a scholarship of knowledge from magazines about the correct books to read and TV shows to watch and albums to own – not just because I enjoyed these things, which I only mostly did, but in case anyone at any time asked me a question about them.

Of course, my suburban surroundings meant that true coolness was always out of my reach. I wanted to go to parties where The Smiths were playing on the stereo, ideally a stereo controlled by a gentle boy in a skinny black tie rolling me a jazz cigarette (which wouldn't affect me, but would make me look fantastic), and all I got was sixteenth birthday parties in my sort-of friend Hannah's garage, full of drunk boys in polo shirts singing along to 'Let's Get Retarded'. Why were the Black-Eyed Peas even allowed to release a song called 'Let's Get Retarded'? I knew I had to go to university in the city.

So I did. At uni, the Anna-Graces wore The Presets T-shirts of and black vintage boots. They had artfully messy hair and exquisitely applied eyeliner. They worshipped the same idols I had been studying in my bedroom for years. They were also fucking mean.

'Can I sit here?' I asked a girl before a literature lecture. I had been eyeing her off as a potential friend for a few weeks. She wore ripped tights, a black leather skirt, a flowy vintage shirt and a beret. I immediately made a mental note: *berets = not bad.*

'Yep,' she said glancing at me quickly then turning back to her phone. We sat in silence. *You've made it this far, keep going!* I thought.

'Hey, thanks for the seat!' I said, reminding her what I was doing there. 'People have been saving seats heaps, which is pretty annoying!'

'Oh, yeah?' she said to my lie. She looked up from her phone and immediately started talking to the person on the other side of her. I considered asking her if she was enjoying uni, but stopped myself. I didn't need to squeeze any more humiliation out of the interaction. I never approached her again.

I was rejected by a couple more cool arts students who looked like American Apparel models, but I befriended some, too. Like them, I started dressing in black mini-skirts and ruffly Victorian blouses adorned with plastic brooches of bats or pins in the shape of Michel Foucault's head (I didn't even really know who he was) (I sort of still don't really know who he is). I met people who knew people who played in popular bloghouse bands. I was photographed in clubs looking at the ground as if I didn't know the photographer was there, but pulling a peace sign so it was an unavoidable fact that I knew they were there. I loved partying, but I also loved peace. I was amazed at how easily I was adapting to this lifestyle.

I told myself that leaving high school behind had meant my 'true self' was finally being unlocked, without considering that I was just following a new set of guidelines that were far more insufferable than the last. I did start going to parties where The Smiths were playing. I knew the words to many Radiohead songs and could prove it. Once, I was listening to 'Mysteries' by the Yeah Yeah Yeahs and my friend said, 'I love Kings of Leon!' and I said, 'No, this is the Yeah Yeah Yeahs,' and she said, 'Oh.' She looked like she wanted to fall into a sinkhole and be incinerated by the core of the earth. I was elated.

It felt like I was finally mimicking an ideal correctly, like I had been studying for this assignment for years and had finally got my High Distinction – until I was confronted with a new hurdle: the kids at university were massively smarter than I was.

These Anna-Graces had read *Howl* in the summer between Year Eight and Year Nine. They knew everything that had happened in the entirety of the Cold War, maybe even stuff the Australian government didn't know. They had posters of William S Burroughs on their walls. They would tell me that, sure, *Less Than Zero* was good, but Bret Easton Ellis' masterpiece was *American Psycho*, and it was okay that I didn't know that – I hadn't read it after all. It didn't really matter that I was turning up to class wearing a giant T-shirt with Laura Palmer's dead face on it and listening to The Shins on my iPod, because I had never read *Infinite Jest*.

They were also mostly rich, which made them somehow more secure in their intellect. They didn't need part-time jobs in chicken restaurants or in clothes shops that specialised in leggings trying to look like jeans. This gave them a sort of carefreeness and a casual, elegant boredom. They would spend their weekends drinking coffee in tiny cafes named after saints and walk listlessly around the city taking photos on analogue cameras that cost thousands of dollars. They lived at home with their families in suburbs that were invented for the purpose of building identical five-bedroom houses that snaked around a fake lake.

'Your bedroom has a bathroom attached!' I said to one uni friend when visiting his home during the summer holidays. He looked at me blankly.

'Yeah?' he said, waiting for the point I was preparing to make after such an obvious statement. I may as well have been saying, 'Your kitchen has a sink!' It was the first time I'd known anyone (outside of characters on *The Nanny*) who had access to an ensuite.

It became clear that without getting a large bucket, putting it in the corner of my bedroom and calling it an ensuite, there was a limit to what I could copy. I was a good student, but I wasn't able to replicate someone else's inheritance or brain.

With graduation looming – along with questions about what I actually wanted to do next, a decision I couldn't look to others to decide for me – I found myself wondering how Anna-Grace had fared. Was she the Anna-Grace of her high school? Did she go to university? Did she read *Infinite Jest*? How would she decide what her career should be? She would've been able to do any job she wanted. Maybe it wasn't that I had wanted her sneakers or to be in charge of the lunchtime games after all; maybe what I had been chasing this whole time was Anna-Grace's trust in herself. I was never sure of anything I had come up with on my own.

The last time I saw her had been the summer that I turned fifteen. She was working at a fast-food Mexican place in the food court of my local shopping centre, her uniform an acid-yellow polo shirt and matching visor. Even though I was in normal clothes (moleskin trousers and some sort of yeehaw shirt from Jay Jays) I immediately hid behind my mother.

'What?' my mum said loudly, whipping her head around while I pretended to be deeply interested in the fluorescent bubbledress display in the window of Supré. If Anna-Grace was wearing an acid-yellow visor and handing out little plastic cups of guacamole, then that was the correct thing to be doing in that moment. It didn't matter that I now knew stuff about trendy music and obscure movies, because I would never have the self-assurance that made people want to copy her in the first place. I was always mirroring other people's tastes; I didn't know how to just *be*.

A few weeks later, in a move that I convinced myself was totally unrelated to any tall and beautiful former acquaintances from the Seychelles, I got my first job: scooping ice-cream at Wendy's in that same food court. I wondered if I would bump into her in the grey labyrinth of corridors that led to the skip, and if she would even recognise me – or just mistake me for a lost child in a stained polo shirt with an ice-cream cartoon on the back.

I never did bump into her. Three weeks after I got the job, a smiling manager at Wendy's told me I had been 'terminated'.

'Oh, cool!' I said, relieved that they didn't need me for my shift. My friend was having a party at her house that night, a house so frequently devoid of parents that I sometimes wondered if she had any. My manager smiled warmly and nodded his head. I smiled back as he handed me my last payslip. I walked out of the shop, smugly waving to Sandra, the other teenage scooper, as I went. *What a sucker,* I thought to myself, imagining Sandra mopping up sticky syrup while I was drinking Smirnoff Double Blacks in a basement. Sandra waved back limply, a slight frown on her face.

It took two whole days for me to realise I had been fired. I wasn't sure why, but the fact that scooping the firm ice-cream was often too strenuous for my twig arms – arms that had never handballed a football or supported my weight on monkey bars or held any trophy of any kind – was probably behind it. Maybe I should have put more energy into copying whatever Sandra was doing.

The best fakes in fiction

Julianne in *My Best Friend's Wedding*

The most impressive kind of faking is when you furiously dedicate every cell in your body to pretending that you are the most chilled-out person to have ever existed. This is what happens in *My Best Friend's Wedding*, which is a horror movie about what happens when a woman has no female friends to tell her that she's being an arsehole.

In this film, Julia Roberts' character, Julianne, is very good at faking being a better person until she is suddenly not. In order to win back an old boyfriend, played by Dermot Mulroney, who's about to get married to Cameron Diaz (this makes Julia realise that she wants to get married to him, or similar; she doesn't want him to marry someone else, in any case, and she definitely needs to get married because she's twenty-eight), Julia needs to pretend that she is the exact kind of relaxed tomboy that men want to marry. This fake personality means that she needs to channel her uptight-food-reviewer tendencies into doing things like very performatively going to baseball games instead of fancy lunches, and carrying no less than four beers at any one time. She also fakes being relaxed by taking every opportunity to set Cameron Diaz up in distressing scenarios and then, when Cameron inevitably gets distressed, pointing at her like, 'Look how she stresses so!'

If Dermot Mulroney wasn't so in love with Cameron Diaz, Julia's fake personality would have been more successful. In the end, she gives up on faking it, but so does Cameron Diaz, who it turns out has also been faking a relaxed personality the whole time. Women are very good multitaskers.

Tom Ripley in *The Talented Mr Ripley*

The second-most impressive kind of faking is the kind of faking that takes you to the Italian seaside. In *The Talented Mr Ripley*, Matt Damon's character, Tom Ripley, does not fake his personality in order to move through the world more easily; he mainly fakes it in order to murder people and to steal their money. He is extremely good at this. He is particularly good at contorting himself to fit the comfort levels of the rich people he is with, making himself a very passive, non-offensive hang who just becomes part of the furniture – which backfires when these rich people eventually decide that he is too much of a suck-up to hang out with long-term.

You see, this is the trick: in this movie, Matt Damon makes himself an agreeable blank space for Jude Law and Gwyneth Paltrow to project onto. He fakes it so well that he *ceases to have a personality.* That's why Gwyneth Paltrow feels comfortable telling him her relationship woes and Jude Law feels comfortable telling him about the mistresses he has impregnated. Matt Damon may be morally bankrupt, but he does a great job of it.

(A warning to all try-hards: your performance won't work if there is even one cynical Philip Seymour Hoffman-esque person in your orbit, so try to surround yourself with brainless millionaires at all times. They will likely be wearing linen and will force you to watch them play the saxophone.)

Hyacinth Bucket in *Keeping up Appearances*

When I saw the 'Red Wedding' episode of *Game of Thrones* for the first time, I remember thinking, *Wow, that is the most devastating piece of television I have ever seen,* but then I remembered it wasn't actually, because there is more pain and humiliation depicted in a single scene of *Keeping Up Appearances* than there is in the entire eight seasons of *Game of Thrones* put together.

Keeping Up Appearances is a British show about a woman named Hyacinth who is from a lower-middle-class background, but who constantly tries to hide this and is terrified that people will discover she hasn't always led a genteel life. She has a northern accent but puts on a posh voice, pronounces her surname like

'Bouquet', often brags about her fancy Royal Doulton china and does things like pretending to go on luxurious holidays to impress her snobby neighbours, who she mostly hates. Her family are normal people, so Hyacinth hates them, too. The message of the show is that everyone should be embarrassed of their true selves at all times.

If there ever is a worldwide class revolution, it will probably be because someone watched a well-timed episode of *Keeping Up Appearances*.

Jean Valjean in *Les Misérables*

Have you ever been told by a bishop, 'Hey, no hard feelings about trying to steal my silver candlesticks, I get it; take them, just please promise to be a better man,' and then thought, *Yeehaw, I'm going to be so rich, I will be the richest and most devilish convict of all time!* but then felt bad about this, so instead changed your identity, took in a beautiful orphan and became a wealthy businessman in a city where people were starving to death? To be a better man? You still build hospitals and stuff? But you're still quite comfortable?

We could learn a lot from that bastard Jean Valjean, is what I'm saying.

Don Draper in *Mad Men*

Most of *Mad Men* is about people pretending to be someone else and worrying about being revealed as a fraud. But only Don

Draper fabricates his entire identity by assuming that of a man he saw die in the Korean War. How enterprising!

Don Draper is so good at faking things about himself that he kind of becomes a mentor to other people who need to hide things about their lives. 'It will shock you how much this never happened,' Don says to Peggy while encouraging her to lie about giving birth to a baby out of wedlock. Peggy, whose job up until that point largely involves lying about Don's whereabouts so people don't realise how many simultaneous affairs he is having, is comfortable with this lie. The only thing that Don Draper can't seem to fake is not being an arsehole, which doesn't matter because he's upsettingly handsome and, well, that's life, folks.

Mulan in *Mulan*

If I could fake being a man for a day, I would probably just try to earn a reasonable wage. The Chinese Imperial Army looks fun, though. A lot more singing than you'd think.

Elena in the *Neapolitan Novels*

One of the best things about Elena Ferrante's four-part series about friendship, love and betrayal across six decades in Naples, is the way Elena the narrator's inner monologue differs from what she actually says to the other characters. Elena does an incredible job of faking her feelings.

Any character: 'Hello, Elena.'

Elena's brain: 'How dare they. How disappointing. Life will never be more than an endless stream of disappointments. My bones are lead. My brain is constricted by hot copper coils. I will never find peace. I will never find comfort. I must perpetually walk barefoot on this path of sharp stones, into the ocean, which will sting my bare skin with salt and icy spray. There will be no relief from this.'

Elena: 'Hello.'

William Miller in *Almost Famous*

William Miller may have given me false expectations of a career in music journalism, but it's not his fault that print started dying by the time I finished high school and then Facebook ruined digital media by the time I turned twenty-five. That's not his fault! Anyway, some people may say that William's earnestness and desire to be accepted by Penny Lane and the band members of Stillwater mean that he was more try-hard than expert fake, but there is one person he successfully fools into thinking that he is someone else: Ben Fong-Torres, the editor of *Rolling Stone*.

William pretends that he isn't fifteen and is actually in his twenties (he puts on a deep voice on the phone) and Ben Fong-Torres is like, 'Sounds good, William, we have never met but here is a bunch of money, please follow Stillwater around the country.' William keeps this going for several months and gets his accommodation and food paid for across the country: just drinking and partying with rock stars, all paid for. *For one story.* I don't even like expensing taxi receipts.

There is a bit in *Almost Famous* when William is on the phone crying to Lester Bangs, who reminds him that it wasn't just the music that attracted William to Stillwater – it's that William wanted to belong, and Stillwater made him feel cool.

'Even when I thought I was, I knew I wasn't,' William admits.

But Lester Bangs says that being cool isn't the most important thing, because you can belong in other ways. 'The only true currency in this bankrupt world is what you share with someone else when you're uncool,' he says.

In the end it turns out that Stillwater aren't really cool either – they're mostly insecure boys who are also just looking for approval. Masculinity is fragile!

Billy in *Scream*

Billy's turn in *Scream* (aka going from being a guy who is dying to a guy who is a psychotic serial killer) is impressive and fraudulent behaviour. Not only does he manage to trick everyone into thinking that he is not a murderer, he also tricks Sidney into thinking he's a nice guy for the length of their relationship. If you're handsome, you can get away with anything.

Sidney is sincerely shocked every time Billy is revealed to be a dickhead (and forgives him for being a dickhead almost every time). To be honest, even if he hadn't just confessed to murder and wasn't holding a knife to her throat at the end of the movie, the fact that Billy was like, 'Hey, Sidney, would you like me to explain some movie references to you, you're welcome, Sidney,' would have been enough. There is nothing worse than a teenage boy explaining movie plots to you. I would have just walked into the knife.

Amy in *Gone Girl*

YOU DIDN'T GUESS THE TWIST, NO ONE DID.

It's a hell of a town

Before I had ever visited New York, I was obsessed with the idea of attending a party there. I longed to see the Central Park-facing pre-war apartments (what war? It didn't even matter) that Nora Ephron wrote about: the doorman standing guard, granting entry to women in cashmere wrap-dresses so they could attend cocktail parties in what I was sure would be tastefully decorated penthouses. It would be perpetually autumn, somehow. For some reason, I couldn't imagine that sequence of events happening in any city but New York.

It wasn't just what happened in those cream-curtained homes: I also spent a lot of time thinking about Studio 54. It's weird that TV pundits wring their hands over rap music and teen TV shows supposedly inciting their kids to ingest large quantities of alcohol and drugs, when there are Studio 54 party photos of Jerry Hall swigging out of a champagne bottle, a glassy-eyed David Bowie staring at a disco ball, and Bianca Jagger holding a live dove, all freely available on the internet.

What on the outside was a plain black building – an unassuming former television studio – was revealed inside to be a glittering, red-velvet palace full of people clad in gold lamé dancing to a Donna Summer DJ set; Bianca Jagger in a ruby-red ball gown, trotting around the dancefloor on a white horse; Truman Capote, Andy Warhol, Debbie Harry and Paloma Picasso sitting at a table, drinking cocktails that probably aren't even available to non-celebrities. I read that on Dolly Parton's birthday, the club was transformed into a farm with hay and live donkeys and live chickens, and Dolly Parton sort of hated it but it didn't really matter. I read that during one New Year's Eve party, they dumped over 3628 kilograms of glitter onto the guests. For months after, people were finding pieces of glitter in their ears and shoes and underwear.

When I was growing up, I spent a long time dreaming of New York, because I had been told by the television that it would unlock a special part of my brain that was creative and dynamic, and that it would change me in ways Melbourne could not. I imagined walking down the same streets as Debbie Harry and Frank O'Hara and Keith Haring and Karen O and Edie Sedgwick and Q-Tip and Patti Smith, and I wondered what bolts of brilliance would shoot up from the cracked pavement into my feet. Some corner of my brain told me that achieving something in America made the achievement matter more – that Australia was too easily conquered. Having achieved nothing in Australia, or anywhere else for that matter, I have no idea where that confidence came from. I was twenty-one the first time I went to New York, with my friends Imogen and Steph. It took me a year and a half to save up the money, even though I was still living at home. By then, I'd been told by LCD Soundsystem that it was already 'over', but I suspected that every generation thought the previous generation got the better version of the city.

If you are an Australian who has moved to New York you will, fortunately or unfortunately, have houseguests from back home for the rest of your life there. What do Americans think of these Australian visitors who filter through in a nervous line like a never-ending immigration queue: people who take a long time to count their change at lunch and snap blurry photos of the big whale in the Natural History Museum and drink warm PBR cans on the street and buy single tacos with unholy enthusiasm? I stayed in the studio apartment of a guy called Chuck, along with seven other people – and that's not including Chuck, who was thrilled that his homesickness was being temporarily abated by a string of visitors who were all sleeping on mattresses on the floor. One of the people staying there was Chuck's mum. She was furious.

I spent days walking the sweltering-hot pavement, jamming every hot dog I saw into my mouth and pointing to fire hydrants while marvelling to whoever I was with that it all looked 'just like in the movies!' – miraculously without being punched once. I spent humid nights sleeping on a blow-up mattress that I had bought, sharing the living-room floor with all the other Australians – some of whom had been promised a private room, all of whom were paying rent – all of us sweating profusely in the un-air-conditioned loft. One night it was so hot that Steph and I ate half a tub of ice-cream each for dinner and finished the rest for breakfast.

I soon discovered New York novelties I had never even imagined: in New York, you can get bacon mac-and-cheese delivered at 3am. You can go to a museum that has a celebrity sex tape exhibition and walk into a room that has a naked Paris Hilton and a naked Colin Farrell and a naked Kim Kardashian projected on the walls and not *really* think about the ethics of that because you're young and your brain is mostly fairy floss and gin. You can get approached on the street by a woman who asks you if you'd like to work at American Apparel. On the summer solstice you can climb up onto a rooftop (it's too hot to go up there during the day; your shoes would melt on the concrete) and watch the sun rise. You can stand outside the Condé Nast building and just stare at it, as if staring will be enough to transport you inside, and maybe you'll be the culture editor at a fashion magazine, and maybe there will be a resurgence of the publishing industry, and maybe the competition isn't *too* bad here, and maybe all these other young women who are standing around also staring at the Condé Nast building want to work in the legal department or in accounts.

It had always felt like being in New York, even for a short time, would inspire me to do something big. But while I was inspired to buy T-shirts and eat a lot of Cuban food, I didn't feel any more creative. When I put my earphones in and listened to 'Reptilia' on the subway, staring out the window as the train sailed into Manhattan, it did feel like a movie, but I wasn't any cooler when the song finished. It seemed like a place that was very easy to visit but maybe very hard to stay. Everyone I knew who had moved there from Melbourne had found it difficult – sure they sometimes saw Ben Stiller on the street, but they were terrified of ever needing to go to the doctor. I didn't have much money at home, but at least I had a Medicare card. I didn't feel bolts coming up from the pavement; mostly I only felt chewing gum.

'More Australians,' I heard one of Chuck's American friends say with a sneer to her buddy, at a rooftop bar he had taken us to. The friend laughed and rolled her eyes. You couldn't blame them: personally I had spent my first couple of days in the city self-consciously buying clothes to make me feel like I could pass as a New Yorker, and then realised that the oversized Opening Ceremony T-shirt and Supreme cap (worn backwards) I'd bought made me look like a tourist anyway.

'Can you not take so many pictures?' Imogen said at the end of our first week, I think because she thought there was a chance that *she* at least could pass as a local. This resulted in her pretending she wasn't impressed by anything that we saw on our trip. I took pictures of fire hydrants and stared at subway maps for far too long, and Steph put INXS on the jukebox at bars, partly because we were homesick and partly because we were rendering ourselves exotic.

One night, the three of us went to a club night in Manhattan that was (allegedly) hosted by Chloë Sevigny's brother, which was the closest thing to a glamorous, celebrity Studio 54-esque experience we could imagine.

'Do you think Chloë will be here?' Steph said, scanning the crowd of people who, quite reasonably, all looked like they could have been extras in *Kids*.

'A guy in the bathroom line gave me a pill!' said Imogen.

The Americans looked at us as if they were watching a particularly sad documentary about Rumspringa.

There was this interview once with one of the founders of Studio 54, Ian Schrager, who said that despite all of the glamour and farm animals and underpants glitter, there was only one thing he felt when thinking about Studio 54: 'embarrassment'.

He probably said this because on the night of 14 December 1978, a bunch of IRS agents raided the club, found giant stashes of money and moderate stashes of drugs, and decided to send the club founders to jail. It probably shouldn't be surprising that the owners were too distracted to focus on business admin. People took a lot of drugs very openly at Studio 54; it was just normal. People flicked their feathered hair out of their face, did a line on a perspex table, then took off all their clothes and performed a spontaneous burlesque dance in a giant cocktail glass. There was also the very unsavoury basement room, where the owners kept old props, mattresses and VIP patrons who wanted to have sex with each other. If you couldn't get in there, there was also the balcony, which contained a 'rubber room' specifically designed to be easily wiped down. In her memoir, Grace Jones said it 'was a place of secrets and secretions, the in-crowd and inhalations, sucking and snorting'. It was a place where you could expand your mental horizons with mind-altering substances, become a shining beam of energy, lose yourself in the thump of disco, fall in love with a beautiful actress or famous intellectual, and if you pissed yourself because you took too many pills, don't worry, this room is made out of rubber.

One time, the Studio 54 owners noticed that there was a weird smell in the club, but this time the rubber room wasn't to blame. It transpired that a man – who didn't want the bother of waiting in line for the club, a line from which even celebrities were sometimes turned away – had put on his finest black-tie attire and decided to sneak in. He had crawled into the club's air vents, where he had gotten stuck and … died. It was several days before they found him, still in his suit. At the last party before the founders were due to start their jail sentence, Liza Minnelli sang 'New York, New York', and everyone who had managed to enter the club through the door cheered.

The night after we attended Chloë Sevigny's brother's club, which turned out to be pretty much exactly like clubs in Melbourne but just a bit more crowded, we went to Katz's Deli – *When Harry Met Sally* territory. I was practically vibrating with joy at the combination of two of my great loves: Nora Ephron and sliced meats. I wanted to photograph everything I saw but refrained to appease Imogen, who was already hungover and thus much more sensitive to my overtly touristy behaviour. I opened my eyes wide and turned my head slowly as if I was taking a panoramic shot, not wanting to miss a detail.

'It's okay,' Imogen said, yawning. 'You can take a photo of the menu.' I smiled and shrugged. I had already stuffed one of the menus in my tote bag. I bought a T-shirt on our way out. Imogen bought a chilli dog that gave her diarrhoea. It was the best trip.

Whose fault is it, though

Do you think it's Hermione Granger's fault? Because she memorised all her text books on the school holidays and was like, 'levi-*OH*-sah' and was insecure about having non-magical parents, but also deeply, no-doubt-in-her-mind secure about her own abilities? That whole Time Turner thing? Being so productive that it bent the rules of *time and space*? That her teachers were like, 'Yes, this thirteen-year-old is too smart to obey minutes; minutes and hours, they are beneath her'? Even your most productive hour will never be as productive as one of Hermione's Time Turner hours. So. Just think about that.

Do you think it's Matilda? Who taught herself to read and had consumed all the classics by the age of four? Who was so profoundly confident of her moral superiority that she thought it was appropriate to dedicate herself to 'punishing' the other members of her family, who were less moral and had probably never read *Moby Dick*? Even her teacher was like, 'Yeah, you are better than your parents who clothe and feed you, 100 per cent'? She could also move stuff with *her mind*?

Is it Jess from *Bend It like Beckham*, who worries about being a good daughter and a good sister and a good friend, and whether she can do all of these things simultaneously while also following her dreams of playing soccer? And she does end up doing all those things successfully *and* smooching a boy, and no one is mad at the end? She has done it all perfectly? Not one *single* person is mad?

Is it The Bride in *Kill Bill*, who was like, 'Yeah, you tried to kill me, yeah, you tried to ruin my life, but guess what? I have the strength of character to endure, and not only endure but become stronger; and I will be emboldened by a desire to reap bloody justice upon you, and I will succeed, and my revenge will be so pure and fair that God himself will swoop down from the heavens and help me drive this stake through your heart'? And she still somehow has time to do Outfits?

Is it Kylie Minogue, who managed to be a mainstream pop princess, then a triple j darling, then a gay icon who soundtracked the dawn of the new millennium all in a single decade? Just transcended all of those social circles like it was easy and fit in everywhere? Now when you go to her shows there are so many different demographics at her concert it's like you're at a funeral for British royalty? (One of the popular ones, not one of the Nazi ones.)

Is it Belle, who was extremely beautiful and extremely clever and who everyone wanted to marry? And who was quite bored 'with this provincial life' and wanted adventure in the great wide somewhere? And so found the meanest, richest 21-year-old in the town nearby and tried to make him over? And proved that mean men become good if you just give them *lots of attention*?

Do you think it was Carrie Bradshaw, who more than once set the precedent that it was a totally reasonable friendship expectation to call people in the middle of the night and say 'COME HERE!' and they would have to do it, even if you had spent the rest of that week yelling at them, otherwise they're a bad friend? And then when you get there, Carrie is like, 'I'm sad about that guy I briefly dated :/ A year ago :/ .'

Do you think it's Ginger Spice?

Look, we have a whole book to work this out.

Iceberg

Do you ever think about those musicians who kept playing their instruments while the *Titanic* was sinking? It's fine if you don't, because I think about them all the time. Were they mildly annoyed that no one seemed to be listening? Weren't any of them like, 'Fuck this, I might just hop on a lifeboat; hold my cello'? These eight men had to memorise 352 songs just in case someone in first class fancied a particular tune, and they ended up freezing in the North Atlantic Ocean because the people who owned the ship couldn't remember to pack enough lifeboats. It must have been fairly frustrating to say the least.

My interest in the dead *Titanic* musicians is peculiar, but not *uniquely* peculiar considering that Australia has not one but two monuments dedicated to them. If this seems strange to you that is because it is strange. The musicians weren't Australian. In fact, there is no obvious tie at all between them and the regional towns in which these monuments stand. In all likelihood, they had never encountered anyone from either Ballarat *or* Broken Hill. At the time of its construction in 1915, *The Ballarat Star* newspaper soberly deemed the dignified Edwardian Titanic Bandstand 'a most fitting tribute, under the circumstances'. The sympathetic people of Broken Hill wanted to build a similar rotunda, but managed to collect less than a quarter of the funds needed. They settled for a single marble column that was criticised by the local paper.

Of the 2200-odd passengers on the *Titanic* only six were Australian, but there's no proof that any of them were in bands. It seems as though, during the conversations about building these monuments, no one said, 'Ah, should we build a tribute to the Australian passengers first? Or make it just a general sort of monument? Not *just* one for these eight celebrity guys?' Or maybe they did, and the people in charge replied, 'No, shut up,' because no other story was as juicy as the musicians story.

On the day the bandstand was unveiled in Ballarat, thousands of people stood in the rain while a band performed what they thought definitively was the last song played as the *Titanic* went down. According to survivor accounts, it was the wrong song.

The story about the musicians is so morbidly fascinating that you can't help but be drawn to the ghoulish glamour of the tragedy – even if it means standing out in the rain just to hear a sad song that's not even a historically accurate sad song. It's the kind of heroic and upsetting story that piques the imagination so much that you start to insert yourself into it and make it your own. And that's why I thought I'd made the whole thing up.

When I was in primary school, I was sure that I was good at creative writing. It was a very nice feeling. Once, in parent-teacher interviews, my Grade Three teacher, Mrs Ryan, asked my parents if I read newspapers, because I seemed to naturally arrange my writing in neat little paragraphs without being told to. My mum and I exchanged a look, silently agreeing to uphold the charade that I read newspapers instead of what I actually did most days, which was read YA novels set in the time of the Potato Famine and avoid social interactions.

That I had been gifted this whole time was a compelling idea for an eight-year-old. I began to believe that maybe Mrs Ryan had seen something in me that I didn't recognise myself: an artistic greatness just waiting to be unlocked. This newfound confidence reached its peak a year later, when I first saw the most exquisitely important film of the 20th century. And it changed everything.

When *Titanic* came out in 1997, people were prepared to hate it. 'It cost 200 million dollars!' morning-show hosts said to each other in disbelief. 'I heard a crew member tried to poison James Cameron!"* Then it came out, and the entire world loved it. When a movie makes the good guys beautiful teens with floppy hair and the bad guy a pointy, murderous chunk of ice, it can unite all kinds of people.

I didn't get to see *Titanic* until a year after its release, when my parents rented the VHS. We rarely rented videos, so I knew I had to concentrate to make it worth it. Even though the 195-minute running time meant that they lost interest in the film very quickly – my dad left the living room to disassemble a bookshelf with his friend Jerry, even though it was past nine at night – I was transfixed. This movie had everything I cared about in a story: danger, death and montages of running to quick violin music. It may not have had the laughs of my first favourite movie at the time, *The Birdcage*, but I understood that Robin Williams could only make so many movies in a year.

It was hardly a surprise that I felt deeply moved by *Titanic* – I had spent the last eighteen months absorbing *Entertainment Tonight* segments and *Herald Sun* lift-outs about the movie,

---

*   That actually *did* happen. In 1996 on set in Nova Scotia, some of the cast and crew of *Titanic* sat down to a midnight meal of clam chowder, which, unbeknownst to them, had been laced with PCP. About half an hour after dinner, crew members started experiencing confusion and other hallucinogenic affects. (James Cameron immediately made himself vomit up his chowder when he realised something was amiss.) A 1997 *Entertainment Weekly* report claimed that 'people were just rolling around, completely out of it'. Can you imagine the scene? James Cameron and Bill Paxton and Old Rose vomiting up clam chowder like they were in a *Monty Python* sketch while staring at styrofoam icebergs in a 64-million-litre tank? Buses rushed the crew to hospital and *EW* ominously warned that 'the culprits are still at large'.

wondering less about what would happen to Rose and Jack than what it would look like when the ice tore the guts out of the ship and everyone started dying. *Heaps* of bad things have happened since the *Titanic* sank, but it's still one of our favourite events to talk about. It's perfectly understandable that it was a big topic back in 1912, because there probably wasn't a huge amount to discuss in those days. It's not like you could hang out in the town square gabbing about the latest *Killing Eve*. All you talked about was the people you knew, and they were probably pretty boring, too, and then you went to bed. (World War I changed that and was pretty solid as far as 'trending topics' go.)

Anyway, this is all beside the point. When I woke up the morning after I saw *Titanic*, I was inspired. I don't think I had ever felt 'inspired' before that moment, or even knew what that meant. Before my sister had woken up, I crept out of our bedroom, our heavy solar-system-print curtains still blocking out the first signs of dawn, and set myself up at the cluttered desk in the spare room, moving aside broken Polly Pockets, my grandad's medical textbooks from the 1960s and stuffed toys I had stashed there so visitors wouldn't know I was a baby.

I'm not sure how long I wrote for. My hands weren't moving fast enough to keep up with the dazzling words and ideas being telecast from my brain. It was a unique piece of fiction, I knew that. I couldn't identify from where this inspiration had come, but I was actually harnessing it and it was exhilarating. This was going to be the best thing I had ever written.

There are many movies about artistic people being frustrated and upset about their lack of creativity, until suddenly they get a sublime burst of it, quickly run to their typewriter/canvas/loom and just create like there are fires of dangerous energy licking their feet. This, honestly and without exaggeration, is how nine-year-old me felt about writing this story. It was finally clear that not only was I going to *be* a creative genius, but I already *was* one – I had talents that other kids my age just didn't have. (When does that confidence disappear, by the way? When I was little, I remember all the girls in my class being pretty sure of their talents – whether that talent was marbles or maths or running or giving dirty looks or French-braiding hair.)

I was so convinced that I had moulded something beautiful, that it seemed perfectly reasonable to burst into my parents' bedroom at 5am on a Sunday and tell them all about it.

My parents, still in bed, eyes blinking in pain and weary disbelief at their incredible misfortune at having such a supremely smug child, listened in silence as I read my story to them in the dark.

My story was about a set of twins and their mother in the early 20th century. These charismatic kids, through great ingenuity and dogged resilience, survived a ship crash on a vessel so grand it was said to be unsinkable. One of the twins was courageous and cheeky, the other studious and kind; it was as if I had isolated what I considered my own best qualities, decided that realistically it was too many good qualities for one person to have and split them up into two people. My story was called *Iceberg*.

Iceberg was short, but filled with fantastical and gruesome detail. There were vivid scenes of the twins being locked down in the lower decks of the unsinkable ship and swimming to find the keys to escape. At one point one of them was handcuffed to a pipe in a room rapidly filling with water. In the reading, I paused for dramatic emphasis every time the twins thought they were about to get away, only to be foiled again by locked gates, missing keys and other screaming children they found abandoned in corridors. 'Help!' I yelled in the final pages, when the twins were huddled on a floating door, waiting to be rescued from the freezing ocean (everyone fit on the door).

In an exhibition of self-restraint that I still don't understand, neither of my parents said, 'Hey, this kind of seems like *Titanic,* that movie we all watched last night.'

'Okay,' my mum said quietly instead, as I bounced out of the room so they could absorb my brilliance in privacy. I knew how my parents would be spending the rest of the morning: trying to figure out how to scrounge up the money to send me to one of those special gifted-child schools like in American TV shows, where I would carry a satchel, learn Latin and develop conservative politics.

'She'll be like Joan Didion!' my mum said, eyes shining and hands resting on her flushed cheeks.

'But wittier!' my dad said proudly, propping himself up on his elbows.

'A tiny Ernest Hemingway!'

'But with greater levity!'

'A baby Dorothy Parker!'

'Yes! Is she the one who does "Effie"?'

'No.'

'Oh, then I don't know who that is.'

This, of course, didn't happen. When a child re-writes the plot of *Titanic* by essentially injecting herself in the movie as two rambunctious twins, it does not strike anyone as particularly clever.

As the years wore on, my confidence in my writing started to evaporate. In Year Seven, I was controversially awarded first place in a creative writing competition, but the vast majority of the class thought that another girl named Emily was the rightful winner. Hers was a profound fictional story about a girl who was writing diary entries about her depression and, in a devastating twist, ended with a last diary entry from her mum saying that the girl had died in a house fire. Everyone in my class cried when they read it.

The story made no sense to me. Why would her mother write an entry in this diary? Was it a magic diary? Most of the stories from the class were about depression or bulimia, or someone who had depression after a long bout of bulimia. Thirteen-year-old girls have very specific interests. My story was about funny encounters with ghosts.

A few years ago I went to the Titanic museum in Belfast with my parents and my boyfriend, Andy. My mum had attended before (my dad had not – he was from the Republic of Ireland and had never set foot in Belfast. He was mildly anxious the entire time) and she was particularly excited to show me 'the ride'.

'Oh, Sinéad, you'll just *love* the ride!' she said to me as we waited in line to enter the exhibition. An elderly couple in front of us looked at each other in concern, no doubt imagining the terrifying hypothermia-inducing drowning simulation that awaited. 'The ride' turned out to be a sort of ultra-slow sit-down escalator that moved through a diorama of scenes of the ship's construction. It was awesome.

We posed for a photo in front of a backdrop of the great ship, as if we were about to ascend the wooden staircase to the deck.

'Should we smile?' asked Andy.

'Yes, because we're not meant to know what's going to happen yet,' said my mum.

I raced ahead and left my family to dawdle around artefacts and 3D displays while I hungrily watched animations of the building of the ship's hub and peered into re-created first-class rooms. I made sure to go through twice so I didn't miss anything, but neglected the audio tour. I didn't think the Irish historian on the tape could tell me anything about the *Titanic* that I didn't already know. I bought a YA book in the gift shop (called *The Girl Who Came Home*, which is a bit of a giveaway) and read it while eating a Titanic Burger, waiting for Andy and my parents to finish their Titanic experience. As I sat there reading, school groups and families jostling around me, I suddenly thought about *Iceberg*.

'Do you remember when I wrote a story ripping off *Titanic* and called it *Iceberg*?' I asked my parents as they exited the exhibition.

'Yes,' said my dad, who I knew didn't remember but who often liked to be agreeable to keep the conversation moving.

'No,' said my mum, turning to Andy and asking him if he wanted a Titanic Burger.

My mum bought me a surprise present at the Titanic Museum. It's important to remember precious times spent with loved ones, we all agreed. It reminds me that I can't judge the people of Ballarat and Broken Hill for wanting their own monument – at least their tribute is somewhat dignified.

The present was a rubber duck dressed as a sea captain with the word *TITANIC* painted on it. It sits proudly next to my twin shot glasses boasting the same logo. I feel no shame.

The perfect woman

I once heard that they changed the recipe for the soft drink Solo because even though the whole point of a fizzy drink is to have fizz in it, people couldn't drink the Solo really quickly without the bubbles burning their tongue and throat. I'm not sure why Solo needs to be drunk faster than other fizzy drinks. Perhaps the creators didn't have enough confidence in the taste of it: didn't think people would want to take a slow sip of Solo, let it pool on their tongues and savour it, shut their eyes in exaltation and then swallow it with an 'Ahhh!' as if they had just sipped the most exquisite nectar from the flower of the universe. Apparently they made it less fizzy, anyway. I don't know if it's true, because I've never looked it up.

In the past, I often took the Solo approach to designing my own personality. (By the by, I think less fizz is a great idea – I remember drinking a Solo during one of my eight ever trips to the beach; my legs were all crusty from sand, and salty air was whipping my fringe around, and I thirstily knocked back the Solo and felt like a Tourism Australia ad.) I longed to be the right amount of fizzy: the sort of woman about whom people would say, 'Oh, I *love* her!' without irony, while exchanging warm smiles and holding wine glasses at the sort of dinner parties you only really see on Instagram. While seeming cool was always a far-off dream, seeming likable didn't just feel like a desirable option – it was the *only* option. I worried about even the smallest social interactions: when I was waking up in the hospital after getting my wisdom teeth out, my first instinct was to make small talk with the nurse passing by my bed, just in case she thought I was being rude.

'I just had a dream about Lindsay Lohan,' I lied, my mouth jammed full of stitches and gauze.

'Oh yes?' said the nurse politely, looking at a clipboard. She didn't mention that you don't really dream when you're under general anaesthetic. 'What was she doing in the dream?'

'Just hanging out,' I replied, dribbling blood.

Whether I realised it or not, I perpetually felt like a walking thermometer, reading the temperature in each room – in each *conversation* in the room – and temporarily lowering or increasing how much of my real self I exposed. Just being authentically nice never occurred to me.

Creating a more digestible version of yourself is easy if you take particular note of your surroundings. It doesn't always work, though. You know that feeling when you're in a too-quiet room and you laugh a bit too loudly? And it sort of rings around the room for a few seconds, every decibel hanging in the air, infused with such awkwardness that you can almost see the sound? And the sound turns into copper coils that seem to tighten around your brain? That's what it feels like when you get it wrong.

I remember being in my early teens, laying on a trampoline with a family friend, pointing at the night sky and saying – in what I thought was a profound voice – 'Look, a shooting star.'

He was silent for a moment, then laughed and said, 'That's an airplane.'

I remember once rolling my eyes and saying 'yes' when someone asked if I had seen *Annie Hall* (I hadn't seen it, I just wanted to seem normal), and then they asked me to tell them exactly what happened in *Annie Hall*.

I remember at my first media job when my cool boss at this pop-culture website said to her cool friend, 'I was an arsehole at twenty-one. Aren't twenty-one-year-olds such arseholes?' They both laughed. One of them was laughing so much she fell sideways on the meeting room couch. I laughed, too.

'Sinéad, what age are you?' my cool boss said.

My 21-year-old armpits started to sweat.

I'd always found that the easiest way to figure out the 'right' kind of behaviour was to look for blueprints to follow, which is why I was drawn to Jo March, the protagonist in Louisa May Alcott's novel *Little Women*. This may sound familiar, because there is likely already a woman in your life who read *Little Women* at a formative age and decided to become a Spirited Woman (or the lady at parties who likes to tell you how she is 'so Jo' when she's had three glasses of pinot noir – which is fairly spirited I suppose). People like that always act as though they are the first person to feel this way. I am not a unique snowflake in my attractions.

Jo is the second-oldest sister in her family, which means she has responsibility but not enough to make her serious. She is funny and bold, talented and fierce, and doesn't have the same interest in romance or balls (the dancing kind *and* other kind) that other girls have. She is ambitious and wants to be rich and famous for writing stories about fantastical murderers. She likes things like ice-skating, which means she is a tomboy. The first time I met Jo was during a teenage viewing of the 1994 iteration of *Little Women*, in which she is played by Winona Ryder.

'I am *such* a Jo!' I would tell my family, as the telly showed Jo putting on her writing cap and scribbling through the night, longing for 'transformation'. This was a not-so-subtle way to communicate to my family that my frequent bouts of rudeness weren't actual character defects, but rather things that just had to be endured from a talented daughter. I made everyone watch it every Christmas.

'Man, I am so like Jo!' I said to Imogen and Steph, as we watched it while Steph's mum cooked us dinner. I casually mentioned how Jo hated the idea of her older sister, Meg, getting a boyfriend and outgrowing their childhood games. *This* was a not-so-subtle way of communicating that I thought our lives should stay exactly as they were – spending weekends with each other, eating chips and going to Blockbuster – instead of what they were slowly turning into, which were weekend-long discussions of parties and the booze we would get for the parties and the boys who would be at the parties.

I decided that I was already so similar to Jo that I should just contort the rest of my personality to be *exactly* like her. I'm genuinely shocked I didn't start wearing hoop skirts, but I guess they weren't available at Jeanswest.

Long before Jo, I had already met other fictional women who provided me with the blueprint of the Perfect Woman I needed to become if I was ever to be valued by anyone at all. Surely I couldn't be liked for who I was. It's fair to say that there was a theme: Kristy from *The Baby-Sitters Club* wore baseball caps and was a small-business owner; Elaine from *Seinfeld* was funny and only had male friends (current me: I literally can't think of anything worse; drop me in a black hole right now; please do an operation on my eyes and ears while I'm awake); Mulan didn't want to get married, so she joined the army instead; sassy Rizzo in *Grease* was hardened and unsentimental and made all the other girls at her high school seem as dull as toilet paper; Lane from *Gilmore Girls* was a rock scholar and so much less wussy than Rory; Éowyn in *Lord of the Rings* fought on the battlefield and said things like, 'I am no man!' while stabbing witch-kings; Winona Ryder in *Heathers* – Winona

Ryder in *anything* – seemed so much more elevated than the ditzy girls around her who only cared about scrunchies and who'd probably never written a poem.

I have never written a poem, but this is beside the point. All of these women eschewed what I thought of as feminine qualities and, because of this, were admired by both men and women and beloved by scores of friends and suitors. For reasons that may have something to do with the fact that I didn't have boobs yet and was terrified of the prospect (don't worry, they still haven't come in), as a kid I never felt like I was a proper girl; I always felt young for my age. Like Jo, I wasn't particularly interested in boys – or girls, or *anyone*, in that way – and only pretended to be interested in them when I sensed that that was the developmental stage I was meant to be up to. I remember queuing up when Chadstone opened a fluorescently lit Toys R Us and brought out cast members from *Neighbours* to awkwardly scribble autographs for pre-teens. I got autographs from Anne (Brooke Satchwell) and Billy (Jesse Spencer). All the girls in my Grade Three class crowded in, carefully passing around the autographed scrap of paper.

'Oh my god, was Jesse Spencer *so* hot?' said my classmate Elena. All the girls looked up at me expectantly.

'Yes,' I said robotically. 'Yes, he was so hot.'

Later that year I stuck a sticker of Billy and Anne on my Write Well exercise book, Billy's blue eyes and white-blond hair glittering like a far-off shore. No one needed to know that

I was just really into their storylines. I still don't think Jesse Spencer is hot.

To my younger self, Jo March encapsulated what I thought were the best attributes of both genders. I wanted to be sentimental and grandiose, but not over-sensitive and weak; coarse but still with the kind of delicate features that would make someone want to scoop me up and take me to their mansion. I had never encountered an instruction manual that explained how misogyny could make me hate certain things about myself or that there were options beyond two genders, and anyway, unless Winona Ryder was explaining it I probably would not have listened. My lack of correct femaleness was offset by my mum's insistence on dressing me up in elaborate garments she had smocked herself: beautiful floral creations that cascaded out in A-line skirts, and which she made me wear whenever other kids invited me out. This resulted in most of the photos of me from the late '90s looking like I was the lost Grand Duchess Anastasia in a sea of denim-overalled children.

I wasn't good at being a girl, which meant I had to try to be good at being a boyish girl – but I wasn't a tomboy and I hated sport, something I presumed was essential for boys. I may not have been interested in clothes or romance, but I was still secretly fascinated by Girl World: a world of powder puffs and glittery eyeshadow and nail stickers. I thought overtly showing interest in these things would be too contrary to the identity I'd been building, so I mostly kept this to myself. This secret passion burned for years, even into high school, where I decided that experimenting with make-up would be a betrayal of my wannabe punk-rock identity.

'You could be pretty, if you really wanted to,' a popular girl called Ariana told me seriously in Year Ten Drama one day (when I retell the story I tend to say that she said 'really pretty', but she didn't – it just makes the stakes higher, as if I was really close; as if I was one GHD hairstyle away from perfection). She looked at my face, tilting her head and frowning as if trying to work out which was the bit about my appearance that I had gotten wrong. Given most of our time together in class involved me and my friends showing off and tackling each other in spirited *commedia dell'arte* performances, I was shocked I was ever still enough for her to notice my almost-pretty face. My friends and I laughed about it all lunchtime – Ariana was a fool! We were intellectuals! I went home and stared in the mirror, studying for the missing puzzle piece to my beauty.

Because that was the thing – I still wanted to be the kind of girl who was beautiful and elegant and who had a pastel-coloured walk-in wardrobe that smelled like baby powder, and had cashmere jumpers stacked on shelves, and BOOTS – so many boots – and a vanity mirror with a padded stool, and a dressing table covered in perfume bottles and little crystal dishes holding earrings and pearls. This sounds like all my fantasies about womanhood were informed by the tastes of the Baroness in *The Sound of Music* (or at least what I imagined her bedroom would be like), which I guess is not far from the truth. (Sister Maria's room was also really nice and velvety and clean but, you know, she felt compelled to turn her curtains into clothes: it was a room too tinged with self-sacrifice.) Jo March hadn't become my blueprint, she had become my identity's parole officer.

It's sort of funny that Jo March became my albatross when she was created in defiance of stereotypes. She wasn't sweet-tempered, she didn't move through social situations with ease, she caused many awkward conversations, she didn't have the kind of beauty and grace that makes great aunts choose someone to take on a trip to Europe. It was weird when she did something as conventional as winding up someone's wife. Near the end of the book, before she ships Jo off for marriage, Louisa May Alcott reminds her readers that Jo is actually a fuck-up: 'Jo wasn't a heroine; she was only a struggling human girl … and she acted out her nature, being sad, cross, listless or energetic, as the mood suggested. It is highly virtuous to say we'll be good, but we can't do it all at once.'

Really, none of my blueprints were that simple: Rizzo gets quite sad about how her tough exterior doesn't allow her to admit that she gets hurt feelings, just like other girls; Mulan ends up dating her boss; Éowyn chases unavailable men and then marries the most emotionally broken man in Middle Earth; Lane gets married at twenty-one and conceives twins the first time she has sex; Elaine loves Jerry the whole time, but can't say. The blueprints contained multitudes, which meant they weren't ever supposed to function as guides but as warm and comforting bursts of energy that would make us feel okay for being too fizzy sometimes.

I went to see the latest *Little Women* movie with Imogen and Steph, now grown-up women with jobs and live-in partners and various early-thirties (emotional and physical) aches and pains. I bawled in a scene in which, on Meg's wedding day, Jo lays her head on Meg's lap and says sadly, 'I can't believe childhood is over.' Several generations of Jos in the movie theatre were crying, men and women who I was sure had also romanticised being difficult, which sometimes involved putting limitations on ourselves and sometimes involved us feeling set free. 'Remember when we were young and you said you were Jo?' Imogen said after the movie, as we were standing around outside the theatre, not quite able to go home. 'Who did we say Steph and I were?'

We all thought for a second.

Steph remembered first. 'I think you said that Imogen was sometimes Meg,' she said. 'But you would also make either of us Beth if you were making fun of us.'

The three of us laughed and shook our heads. It felt nice. We were so different yet so forgiving of each other's sharp edges, which sometimes scraped up against each other. That friction was what made relationships interesting.

'Funny how you always made yourself the main character,' Imogen said, raising her eyebrow at me.

I'm such an Amy.

The heart

'All good things must come to an end but that craving to be loved by everyone you meet will never end, okay, have a nice day.'

—*Charles Dickens, probably*

The Trick

When you are heartbroken and between the ages of twenty and twenty-three, you must take to Europe;* you must pack your scratchy vintage blouses and experimental headwear, your thermals and your large floral passport wallet, photocopies of your bank card, tiny bottles of conditioner and at least one pair of shoes that you will never put on for the entire duration of your trip, because you hate them. You must pre-book planes and trains and hostels on a credit card that will never forgive you, because the idea of just booking things on the road is the choice of someone with courage and spontaneity and four piercings on each ear and natural highlights and loose morals, who only travels with carry-on luggage. You must only go with someone who you know will be able to stomach these behaviours or at least have the decency to hold it in until you find a wi-fi hotspot, where they

---

* I don't actually believe that everyone has the ability or inclination to take to Europe, I just sometimes like to pretend I have strong and definitive beliefs like the Dowager Countess in *Downton Abbey*.

can vent to your mutual friends over chat about how you insist on getting to the airport three hours early or how often you remind them that you're a 'bad sleeper'.

My friend Louise and I had planned our one-month trip to Europe almost six months in advance, and the closer the holiday got, the more strained the threads holding together our respective relationships became. By the time we boarded our flights, we were both single (I had been dumped by someone who said casual things like, 'Do you even have a natural writing voice, or do you just copy the websites who pay you?') and the tone of the trip began to shift. This was originally meant to be a PG-rated cultural exploration that would put us in reasonable debt, a supercut of us at renowned museums and ancient monuments and overstuffed vintage stores and dimly-lit restaurants that sold big bowls of cheese-laden pasta and piles of fresh buttery rolls and endless heavy stews. *Keep it coming, garcon! We're trying to set a record here.* But now that we were single … did this have to be a *Girls Gone Wild* trip? Did we have to stay up all night and do body shots and hang out in the communal area of the hostel and talk to strangers? Did we now have to collect romantic anecdotes like trading cards, so when we got home and people asked, 'So … did you meet anyone?' we could do a PowerPoint presentation of our conquests' profile photos, so no one felt bad for us?

The main issue was that because we both had been in relationships since we were eighteen we didn't really know what being single at home involved let alone being single in Europe, where old men called out to you on the street asking for a date. Louise (who looked like a cross between Marissa Cooper and Rory Gilmore) definitely had more expertise in this area than me (who looked like a cross between a Muppet and a sort of female Frodo Baggins), but neither of us could deny that we'd never really been in a situation where we had actively pursued boys before. They had just sort of been around – boys who we had crushes on and never approached, or boys who we had no interest in and whose company we accepted anyway. Suddenly we were confronted with the fact that we were entering a world of endless possibilities, with different social codes to grapple with – and we needed to prepare. It was because of this, that we invented The Trick.

I can't remember the exact moment Louise and I created The Trick, but it was probably one of the nights we smuggled a bottle of Oyster Bay from Tesco into the private room of our London hostel. We needed to figure how to signal to any romantic prospect that we were interested, giving the green light without the risk of being brutally rejected by someone who was two rungs higher on the hotness ladder. The Trick sounded so simple, so obvious, that we were too embarrassed to explain it to our friends when we got home.

First, you find someone who you find passably attractive. Then you make eye contact with them. Then you *sustain* eye contact with them, and if they don't look away, you smile. That's it, that's The Trick.

Some of you might be reading this and thinking, *Is this dipshit serious, of course smiling at someone conveys that you like them.* But it had honestly never occurred to me to make eye contact with someone I was interested in. I spent so much time avoiding eye contact with people that the idea that it could be used positively, in a non-interrogation scenario, was completely unfathomable. We both decided it was imperative that we try The Trick out in public immediately and congratulated ourselves for being so wise beyond our years, cheersing with plastic cups of contraband wine from New Zealand.

At the start it almost felt like a game. We would squeeze into denim mini-skirts and high-waisted skinny jeans over our thick thermals and go out to bars at night, where one of us – well, Louise – would whisper, 'I'm going to try The Trick.' Just the idea of The Trick emboldened us to be more social with strangers, more spontaneous and eager to see where the night took us – like we were characters in *Lost in Translation* or *Dude, Where's My Car?* Sometimes this newfound friendliness backfired – we played pool one night with two Chilean backpackers who invited us back to their dorm room for drinks, but when we got to the room, there weren't any drinks.

Only an acoustic guitar.

'Do you like … Jason Mraz?' one of the Chileans said, in a thick accent.

'No,' Louise said.

After several minutes, we finally found a musical act that we could all agree on: Radiohead. One of the Chileans grabbed the guitar and began to sing Radiohead's 1993 single 'Creep' – or a version of 'Creep' that just involved yelling, 'I'M SO FUCKING SPECIAL,' again and again while the other Chilean closed his eyes and rhythmically tapped his hand on his thigh. I wondered if they'd packed a guitar on their trip for this specific purpose. How many countries had this poor guitar been dragged through? Did the Chileans take it in turns to haul the sad guitar onto cramped trains, planes and shuttle buses, specifically so we could sit in a small room in London, surrounded by unmade bunkbeds, listening to one of them play 'Creep', the least erotic song of all time? We learned that night that part of being spontaneous and social was knowing when to abandon a situation.

The unfair reality was that Louise didn't really need The Trick. Boys were drawn to her as to the protagonist of a perfume ad. One night in Rome, we went to a bar described in Lonely Planet as the hangout of 'millionaires and their supermodel girlfriends' – as if a place like that would be open to people who took bar advice from a Lonely Planet. We put on dresses that exposed our arms, drank giant gin and tonics and watched a beautiful blonde lady who we thought might be a model. Not long into the night, a young Italian man in a suit offered to drive Louise and me back to our budget hotel. Louise wasn't interested in him, but accepting a lift home seemed like something that could turn into an adventure. We got into his red Porsche – she in the front seat, me squished in the back like a slightly inebriated, bare-armed child – and the Italian man whizzed us down narrow laneways and around tight corners. He was pressing buttons on the stereo and yelling across to Louise.

'DO YOU KNOW FRANK SINATRA?' he asked her.

Louise said that yes, we had him in Australia, too. I rolled my eyes all the way home.

He offered to take Louise on a tour of Rome the next day. She did not take him up on it.

Our faith in The Trick was sustained because of one encounter: the kind of meeting that seemed like it could only happen in Jason Mraz songs. We were in Paris, the second stop of our trip, spending the afternoon in Shakespeare and Company bookstore. I was thrilled to be somewhere so culturally significant, to stand on the same creaky floorboards as F Scott Fitzgerald and Ernest Hemingway and Jack Kerouac had. I wore a tartan scarf. Everything felt so *right*. I absentmindedly slipped a postcard with an illustration of the shop into my tote bag, thinking I could put it up on my bedroom wall at home; perhaps I could look at it while typing out my own great work. Several hours later, I would look at the postcard and realise that it was marked on sale for one euro. While I was shoplifting, Louise was weaving between bookcases and using The Trick on a boy so floppily handsome that he could have been the bad guy in a '90s teen movie. The boy completely avoided the unblinking gaze she shot out at him between gaps in the philosophy section. As we were leaving the bookstore, I congratulated her on the attempt – you couldn't win them all, but it was important to put your hat in the ring. We were half a block away when the boy came bolting out of the bookstore and ran in front of us.

'Hello,' he said.

'Hello?' we said in confusion.

His name was Christian and he was from Austria. He was in Paris studying art or architecture or something else. He asked Louise if she wanted to go on a date with him. Louise seemed to have temporarily forgotten how to speak and just stared at him blankly, as if he was some sort of Hot Boy hologram. I told Christian that Louise *would* like to go on a date with him, as a matter of fact, and provided some paper to get his phone number. We immediately ducked into a restaurant – Japanese; by that point our attempts to digest large quantities of cheese wasn't having pretty results – and Louise, waves of shock radiating off her, nibbled tempura quietly while I sloshed pints of Asahi all over myself and crowed over the success of The Trick.

Christian and Louise went on a few dates in our five days in Paris, one involving her going to an abandoned hospital with him and his friends, an invitation I declined without considering that my friend probably wanted some company while visiting a location that screamed 'grizzly tourist murder'. There was a little part of me that was scared of the possibility of my own romantic encounter. So far my only successful interaction with a stranger had been with an American girl who wanted to take a photo of me in Versailles for her style blog, though in retrospect it was probably less that my outfit was nice and more that the juxtaposition of an extremely cheaply dressed person standing in an ornate room made for an interesting photo.

If you are of a certain age and have a decidedly fanciful disposition, travelling to Europe doesn't just hold the promise of photos in front of the Eiffel Tower and shopping at exotic stores that you don't have back home, like 'Topshop' and 'H&M'. It offers the possibility of transcendence. Maybe you'll hop off your tour bus and buy a villa in Tuscany, where your pregnant best friend, Sandra Oh, can live with you while you reflect on your respective divorces. Maybe you'll visit your Greek relatives and meet a boy called Kosta who is so handsome that it comes as no surprise that your families are currently engaged in a blood feud (you will only ever find your truest enemies to be that handsome). Maybe you'll meet Julie Delpy on a train to Budapest. Maybe you'll meet Timothée Chalamet in Lombardy. Maybe you'll travel to Florence with Maggie Smith and be kissed in a field of barley. Movies taught me that Europe, with all its sophistication and cigarette smoke and large stone buildings that are so much older than the buildings I knew back home, could help me momentarily escape myself and become a better version, one with moxie and luck and a blow-dryer. European me would be bold. European me would get what she *wants*.

As our trip was drawing to a close and the prospect of returning home loomed – to sweltering offices and boring BBQs and a thousand only slightly varying questions about whether any European at all had wanted to kiss me – I knew that I had to follow through and try The Trick properly at least once, just to say I had done it. I didn't want to be like old lady Rose from *Titanic*, regaling depressed people with stories about how I almost had a great and enduring romance – if only I had not let that person, quite literally, slip out of my grasp.

'I have to do it soon,' I told Louise, while we were sitting in a diner eating currywurst and chips for breakfast. It was our last day in Berlin. I was running out of time.

I needed to do it in the next hour. I needed to get it *done*. I needed to wait for a moment when Louise wasn't standing next to me, inadvertently acting like a live action 'before and after' montage. My delay in utilising The Trick wasn't just down to lack of confidence, though saying that I'm lacking in confidence has the same energy as saying, 'Humans need air to live,' and '*Hey Hey It's Saturday* probably shouldn't have come back.' I also just hadn't seen any boys who I was truly interested in. They were either too handsome or too old or too smirky. That is, until that last chilly morning, about an hour after we'd left the cafe.

Do it now! my brain screamed at me when I spotted, for the first time on the trip, a guy who I sort of liked – a dark-haired boy dressed in a button-up shirt and cardigan, holding a tote bag tightly to his body and shuffling quietly across a sombre, crowded street in Converse sneakers. Louise had gone to the bathroom. The boy was headed in my direction.

I can't do it now! I shouted back to my brain, in a more urgent imaginary voice. *Not here, not like this!*

My face twitched into a sort of grimace, my gaze still fixed to the pavement. I saw the Converse boy approaching me, a boy-shaped blur in my periphery. I knew if I wanted to try The Trick, this was it. But I didn't raise my eyes. I couldn't do it. I *wouldn't* do it. Suddenly he was out of the cloudy corner of my vision; the moment was gone. It may have been my last chance to try The Trick, but outside the Jewish Museum in Berlin didn't seem like the right place.

'Yeah, that was probably a good call, hey,' Louise said later that night. We were on our way to a *Twin Peaks*-themed bar, trudging through snow in our denim miniskirts and layers of thermals, to meet a friend from back home. At the bar our friend Beck introduced us to two of her friends – an American who was her boss and whom she secretly harboured a painful passion for, and an Englishman who kept saying very strange things and then getting flustered and apologising a lot.

I had one of those nights where you're incomprehensibly much wittier and more interesting than you are ordinarily. I understood every reference to *Twin Peaks* and said outlandish things about Tarantino movies and Daft Punk albums that no one contradicted. I always had a comeback. I had almost tried The Trick; now I could finally relax.

The more charismatic I became that night, the more the Englishman said things that he immediately seemed to regret.

'This is an extremely creepy corridor,' I said to him, as we both walked the pitch-black path that led to the bar's bathroom.

'I know, it feels dodgy,' he said, before lifting his arms and curling his hands into fake claws. 'Look out, I'm a rapist!' he said in a spooky voice. Before I said anything, he dropped his arms and shook his head in disappointment, apologising for making a joke about being a rapist and assuring me that he actually wasn't a rapist. When I got back to Australia, we continued to message each other for months.

The American, meanwhile, had fallen in love with Louise. He told her stories about how Baltimore rapper Spank Rock was a good friend of his. He bought us tangy alcoholic tea that I later threw up. Louise and the American kissed, and Beck watched, open-mouthed from the corner of the club. As our 6am flight time to Abu Dhabi approached, we said goodbye to our new friends. Beck and I hugged; I thanked her for a funny night that would make a good story for people back home. Beck nodded, smiling, then hugged Louise. As they embraced, Louise's smile faded into a strained look that I couldn't quite read.

'What's wrong?' I said, as we were walking to our hostel, our boots crunching on ice. Louise was frowning, picking at bits of her 3am souvlaki.

'When we hugged, Beck whispered to me, "You've ruined my life, never come back",' said Louise.

Maybe I should have taught Beck The Trick.

Ways I have fantasised exiting a situation

Raising one fist to the sky like Sailor Moon and, mid-conversation, levitating into the air with a *bwamp bwamp bwamp* until I fly directly into the sun.

When I am embarrassed about not being charming enough, melting into a puddle like Alex Mack and then slithering away for many kilometres until I find a body of water to join and then just live out my remaining days there.

When someone has the kind of opinion that's like, 'You know, *hypothetically* …' suddenly concentrating all my energy into creating a sinkhole underneath me – not one that will swallow the person who I'm talking to as well, just a one-person sized sinkhole; we can't get stuck down there together – and then just falling into the cracks of the earth and being incinerated by the earth's core but in a way that tickles.

Just fading into a wall, but no one notices.

Standing in a circle of people I don't really know and then very seriously whispering to someone standing opposite me, 'I have diarrhoea.'

When I have had enough of people for the day, just abruptly stopping mid-sentence and freezing my whole body like I am a mannequin, and just staying like that while the people around me look at each other and say, 'What?' and 'What is happening?' and my arm is outstretched and frozen, and they poke my face to see if I move and then eventually lose interest and move away to talk to a living mobile human, because conversation shouldn't be that much work.

Being asked a question I am not prepared to answer or being confronted with a lie that I have told (that I have heard of a specific band, that I am an astronaut etc.) and then folding my body like a crumpled napkin and dropping to the ground as if I have fainted. It will be so tragic that no one will question me about not being an astronaut ever again.

Seeing someone I know on the street and nodding and smiling and then softly saying, 'Oh!' and jerking my hip like something has made it quiver and grabbing my phone quickly and saying, 'Hello?' so I can save myself and the street person from having to think of things to say to each other. Keeping the phone to my ear for at least another block, making concerned faces and saying 'yeah?' every thirty seconds.

Leaving a venue without saying goodbye to anyone.

Realising that the situation I am in is not actually as romantic as I thought it was and just turning into a pot plant.

Let me down, baby

A world-weary philosopher once said about the object of his affections: 'She's so beautiful that when you look at her your knees tremble, your heart melts and you know, without reservation, that there is order and meaning to the universe,' later confessing that he didn't even need this adoration returned, saying, 'The simple act of being in love with you is enough for me.'

Pacey Witter from *Dawson's Creek* was my first model for the ideal man. Pacey is a character who is bad at school, wears bowling shirts and lost his virginity against a tree to his English teacher. You can see the appeal. According to dawsonscreek.fandom.com, he 'uses humour and sarcasm to relate to people, as well as to hide his emotional pain stemming from his very unhappy childhood'. Fucking sign me up!

I wasn't allowed to watch *Dawson's Creek* because my mum thought it was 'inappropriate', although watching *90210* and *The Martin Short Show* was apparently totally fine for my still-forming brain. Later I found out that 'inappropriate' was just my mum's code for 'this is super boring and I can't be bothered watching it', and it did come as a surprise to me to learn years later that, no, there was not any overtly sexual content in *Sabrina the Teenage Witch*.

As a pre-teen I had a powerful feeling that *Dawson's Creek* was something I needed to be involved with. I bought the soundtrack on cassette and tried to imagine what scene each song was scoring in the lives of these sexy, eloquent teens. I obsessively pored over articles in *TV Hits* that detailed the storylines, taking special interest in an investigative feature on Joey and Pacey's courtship leading up to the episode of them having sex, a relationship's natural end. I used these guides to memorise lines from the show so I could pretend I watched it. I put posters of the cast on my walls, only rotating them once, when my little sister became convinced that a picture of Katie Holmes was following her around the room with its eyes.

I also spent a lot of time contemplating Pacey. Even as a particularly immature ten-year-old who wasn't really capable of having crushes yet, I knew there was something about Pacey. It was Pacey who introduced me to the irresistible concept of yearning for someone from afar. He planted a seed in my brain that said it was possible – in fact probable – that I would have a roguishly handsome enemy/best friend who I had never really thought about in that way, who had loved me all along and who, in the spaces between our verbal sparring, actually thought I was the best thing to have happened on this planet. Heterosexuals are the worst. The longing was a big part of this for me – his longing, not mine. Eventually I would finally flick the hair out of my eyes long enough to see that this boy who loved me actually had a cute face, and it would feel fantastic, like taking ecstasy, a drug I have never taken because it is illegal.

A fictional crush really is the best kind of crush because it relieves you of the pressure of having to perform any unfamiliar and frightening acts of courtship. A fictional crush can never not reply to your texts – they don't have phones or hands! They can never decide they prefer your more attractive friend who has nice teeth – they don't know your friend, she's not part of this! They will never ever pressure you into having sex – they don't have … stuff!

Pacey was an attractive prospect for several reasons. He had a certain ease about him. He always knew the cool or funny thing to say in a situation. He defended his friend Jack against a homophobic teacher. His dad hated him because Pacey never had to fight in the Vietnam War, which meant that Pacey was spoiled. (By the time that Pacey turned eighteen, there weren't any wars available.) His mum was only in one episode so it's unclear why she hated Pacey, but she also powerfully hated him. Pacey recognised when Joey wore her dead mother's bracelet to the prom. He built a boat and then named that boat *True Love*, which should be pathetic and creepy but somehow wasn't because Dawson seemed to monopolise all the pathetic and creepy in the show. Pacey bought Joey a wall, and no I *will not* explain that to you, because if you don't know how important it is to buy a woman a wall, well I'm sorry, good luck being alone forever, you heartless disaster.

Pacey's gentle nature was attractive, but it was the *funny* thing that got me. Pacey ignited my desire for the Funny Guy. Wait, you can understand my witty reference and follow it with another witty reference? You're my crush. Make me laugh once? Fantastic, here are all of my belongings and the deed to at least one of my kidneys. Once I have given you all my money and credit cards and electronics, and am forced to quit my writing career because I'm trying to work on a rock with letters painted on it after I *gave* my laptop to you, you will be mine.

The funny, hot-in-the-right-light, best-friend character would haunt me for many years. 'Him?' my friends would ask when, as a teenager, I pointed out a guy at a party who had made a single joke-ish comment but was otherwise entirely unremarkable. I wouldn't ever pursue them, but I would entertain the fantasy that they had secretly liked me for years and, like Pacey, they were just waiting for the right time to divulge this (just FYI: asking you to get out of a car and grabbing your face and kissing it because you don't care what Dawson thinks is a great time).

My picks for friend-turned-soul-mate were occasionally conventional. As a teenager I had a long, lingering crush on a boy named William who went to a neighbouring school. He was tall, handsome and polite. He wasn't a noted athlete or overwhelmingly cool, but he was still wildly popular with all the girls I knew, because he had never said anything threatening or degrading in front of us. He showed me base-level kindness (he always remembered my name) and once told me that I was funny. These two facts were enough to fuel a full-blown, three-year-long crush on him. At a party in Year Eleven, he asked me to sit on the front lawn with him, because 'he had something he wanted to talk to me about'. We went outside and Sixpence None the Richer started playing in my head.

As we sat down on the grass, he tilted his head and looked at me with a lazy smile. 'There's something weird I want to talk about that I think only you will understand,' he said.

I let out something between a laugh and a gurgle, like I was choking on my own vomit.

He smiled coyly. 'Do you know if your friend Rebecca likes anyone at the moment?' he said, quickly. 'I've liked her for so long and I need some tips on how to win her over.'

For a second – or whatever is shorter than a second; that is a google I can't be bothered doing – I felt as if the earth was crumbling beneath me, and my body was plummeting into a space vortex of nothingness. The next second, I was elated: William wanted *my* advice! This was the best moment of my life. At every party for the rest of the summer we would discuss his progress, with him occasionally giving me a thumbs up from the corner of the room. 'The simple act of being in love with you is enough for me,' Pacey had said, but I started to wonder if that was true.

I don't know when, but at some point the fantasy warped and buckled, and instead of anticipating that platonic friends and acquaintances might secretly be longing for me, I realised that I was the one doing the yearning. No secret admirers were coming out of the woodwork, in any case. Maybe I actually *was* the Funny Guy – the friend who was just waiting for my moment, patiently playing my cards right until the object of my affections discovered how charming I was, then fell in love with me despite the discrepancies in our attractiveness/social standing. It sort of made sense: I believed I wasn't conventionally attractive, but I was sarcastic in a funny sort of way. I thought that maybe, if I fixated on people who were far out of my league, I might be able to wear them down with the sheer force of my unspoken adoration. It didn't occur to me that this is the same strategy used by stalkers, and by bad guys on *Law & Order: SVU*.

As a frame of reference, almost all of the music I was listening to in this era confirmed that if you liked someone creepily enough, they would eventually love you back. Franz Ferdinand taught me how to time every journey to bump into you accidentally; Aqualung helped me imagine putting a 'spell' on you so you'd wake up and suddenly be in love with me; Kings of Leon said that the true love way was to work awful hard for someone who said mean things to you; The White Stripes suggested hypnotising your crush over the telephone; Death Cab for Cutie advised that if only you could see the potential of you and me, then I would possess your heart. If anyone who

146

is aged twenty-eight to thirty-five would like to start a class action against indie bands of the early- to mid-2000s to pay our therapy bills, then I am in.

As a result of adopting the role of Funny Guy, the majority of my teenage romantic interactions involved staring meaningfully at various males who didn't know I existed, while being too chickenshit to let my feelings be known: handsome, witty co-ed-school boys who preferred rich girls with symmetrical faces and big houses; scruffy skaters who were so bored with being stared at that it didn't even register; many boys in many inconsequential bands; and trendy men in skinny jeans who I had fantastically charming shouted conversations with over The Strokes songs before they wandered off to make out with beautiful MySpace girls who only drank Jägerbombs. I was able to lay the groundwork for friendship, but never brave enough for my face-grabbing, Dawson-defying moment.

Sometimes I did make out with boys at parties, not because I liked them particularly, but because they were there and it seemed like the normal thing to do. The boys I was interested in never seemed to be the ones interested in me, but as for the others, it almost (as fucked up as it sounds) felt like it would be impolite to turn them down. In a way, I think this was Seth Cohen's fault.

If you have never watched *The O.C.*, Seth Cohen is a rich boy who has never had a friend until his dad brings home a poor boy whose previous home was jail. Seth plays video games and makes sarcastic jokes to his parents, because he doesn't talk to anyone who is not his parents. (He is unkind to his parents.) He has Ramones and Ben Folds posters in his room and a guitar that we never see him play. He likes Death Cab for Cutie and other indie-rock music that you can find on *The O.C.* soundtrack. He has been in love with a popular girl called Summer since he was ten and names a boat after her (these characters always have boats, because teenage girls find large bodies of water mysterious and sexual). He pursues Summer diligently even though she is not interested in him, and then she decides that she *is* interested in him because he is the first boy who has ever apologised to her.

Seth Cohen reinforced similar things to Pacey Witter – that an unlikely, handsome Funny Guy in your orbit secretly worships you – and now that I was a little older, I became obsessed with him to the point of distraction (spending forty minutes of 'homework time' trying to get my dial-up internet to work so I could check the quotes section of *The O.C.* website). But compared to Pacey, Seth was a lot more neurotic, much less gentlemanly, and his yearning materialised as entitlement – all of which I could forgive because he said funny things and liked good bands.

I don't want to say that the character of Seth Cohen led to some of my worst romantic decisions – including but not limited to agreeing to be someone's first kiss because I felt bad for them; willingly dating someone who regularly got blackout drunk and spoke to me like half of my brain was missing because they were well-read and wore cardigans; and agreeing to go out with a friend who had replied, *Great, want to go out sometime?* when, heartbroken, I had texted him that I had been dumped the week before – but it's not outside the realm of possibility.

Seth is the Funny Guy who also doubles as the Nice Guy, a nerdy man who is entitled to your love because he loves you so much. On the whole, Seth treats Summer quite badly: once he wins her affections, he often lies to her, semi-cheats on her, dumps her without an explanation and sabotages her other relationships because he thinks he loves her more than anyone else can, because he has loved her the longest.

This archetype isn't new. I wonder how many women in history have based their romantic decisions on problematic depictions of the Nice Guy in TV/movies/books/radio-plays. I can imagine a group of girlfriends all sitting around a loom in 1868, discussing how Teddy from *Little Women* made them rethink turning down their neighbour's marriage proposal. 'I mean, I don't find him attractive and we really are more friendship material than anything else, but he does *really* like me and he did ask?' they would say to each other, while scratching their smallpox-ravaged skin and sucking on cocaine lozenges to ease their toothaches. In fact, Teddy is the cautionary tale: if you don't accept the love of a Nice Guy, he will make your least-favourite sister rich, and you will have to marry an old German professor who tells you that your writing is mediocre.

My warped view of the rules of attraction isn't Seth or Pacey's fault, but it's also not *not* their fault. I wonder what my teenage years would have been like if romance hadn't been modelled to me as a tussle in which affection needed to be earned or proven to a reluctant party. Look, I had pretty poor judgement, so I probably still would have kissed that guy just because he gave me two cans of bourbon and coke on New Year's Eve 2005. But it does make me wonder.

It wasn't all a bummer, though. When I think of Pacey and my younger self being thrilled by the idea that my friendship (my personality!) could cause someone to fall in love with me, it seems sweet. The experience of yearning was enough for me. I was in charge of the fantasy, could read into as many texts and across-the-room winks as I liked, and could soundtrack it to whatever CD I was listening to on the bus that day. I put a high premium on loving boys from a distance, boys who, in retrospect, I specifically picked because I was sure they would never love me back. This was safer – I wouldn't need to know what to *do* with all of that.

It's at this point that I need to make a confession. Pacey may have been my first model of the ideal man, but there was actually one before. One who is less socially acceptable, but probably had the same level of influence. And that person was Alan Alda playing Benjamin Franklin 'Hawkeye' Pierce in the seminal 1970s comedy *M*A*S*H*.

Hawkeye, like Pacey, is a lovable rogue who makes plenty of jokes and plenty of noble sacrifices. He wears either a Hawaiian shirt or bloody scrubs, depending on the time of day. He is often drinking martinis, which is fine for doctors in warzones; the 1950s were like that. But unlike Pacey, he also spent a lot of time sexually harassing his colleagues, something that happened in workplaces in the 1970s and hasn't happened once since. There are many parallels between the two crushes, except one is obvious and the other maybe means that I require more therapy.

My love for Hawkeye was more an admiration than a crush, really. I liked him in a way that I didn't fully understand, like praying and hoping that I would get a Furby but then not really knowing what to do with it once I got it. It was a milquetoast attraction, as sexless as John Farnham's 1988 song 'Two Strong Hearts' and as comforting as John Farnham's 1988 song 'Two Strong Hearts'. I think, really, I just wanted to be like him – bold and brave, charming and warm. Maybe all along – with all of these ideals – it was about the fantasy of being confident enough to get the one you wanted in the end.

So, to Pacey Witter, Seth Cohen and Hawkeye Pierce: I forgive you for the fucked examples you set me. I forgive you for both elevating and dashing my expectations of teenage boys all at once. I forgive you for making me vulnerable to the charms of the Funny Guy who, sometimes, isn't always that nice. Luckily for me, in real life there aren't that many funny men out there. Thank god for that.

Parties change

The thing they don't tell you is that parties change when you get older. You have this idea that once you graduate from sticky floors and vodka in plastic cups and private talks in the bathroom and noise complaints from your wealthy neighbour, Sigrid Thornton, and the most confident and least talented man waiting exactly one hour before searching for the aux cord (only then to play 'Hypnotise', which has already been played), you'll suddenly get invited to sophisticated dinner parties every weekend where everyone is drinking tempranillo and saying thought-provoking things, and the apartment is scented like linen and figs and is washed in a warm orange light. Big wooden bowls of pasta materialise from nowhere and there are delicate salads of shaved pear. Somehow there is never a mess to clean up. Everyone is wearing white trousers.

There's a stop between these two kinds of parties, though.

When you get older, the people you know will stop throwing the aux-cord, sticky-floor events because they don't want you to fuck up their apartment or that mid-century ottoman they bought through Afterpay. 'I miss *house parties*,' your friends will still say to each other, remaining unwilling to throw a house party themselves. 'I miss *dancing*.' You will repeat this same conversation with each other every two to three months. Music festivals involve dancing, but you don't really go to many of them anymore either. You're in this suspended animation of not knowing how to have a good time, because all the ways you used to have fun belong to someone else now.

It's not even necessarily a single thing or an in-a-relationship thing, though I'm happy to be corrected. It's almost like, as you get older, your capacity for nonsense diminishes. Your jug is pretty full and you don't want to upset the jug with too many random splashes, otherwise your jug overflows and water gets everywhere and the glass smashes and the dog barks and the fire alarm goes off, and – it's just less important to meet strangers, is what I mean. (Unless you empty the jug completely and start again, which is always an option.) Your next kiss is more likely a friend of a friend or met through an app than a stranger who happened to stand next to you at a club.

But that's beside the point. What I'm saying is that there's a stage where no one has the time or money or inclination to throw dinner parties yet.

So what happens instead is that you hang out in a bar (not a club; you can't talk in a club, and anyway, no one wants to risk not getting into a venue that they used to go to weekly ten years ago) and if everyone is feeling particularly rowdy afterwards, you go back to someone's house. There are never more than eight people in this scenario and there has to be at least three people who agree that 'one more drink' is a good idea, otherwise it won't happen. These people are usually the most charismatic people you know or the ones who work too hard during the week and don't really know how to fix that.

After a couple more drinks, a makeshift dancefloor may begin in the middle of the living room. You will inevitably end up listening to songs that you used to dance to in the first three years after you graduated high school. Suddenly, there are six people over thirty dancing in a circle to a MSTRKRFT remix, and you forget to be embarrassed about it. In the morning, you remember to be embarrassed.

The talk

When I got a job writing for a comedy show it was confronting, partially because I had never done that before and it was quite a vulnerable feeling, and partially because saying that you 'write for a comedy show' sort of feels like you're saying, 'I'm so funny that people should pay me to do it; don't you agree?' It's just a strange claim to live up to.

People had paid me to make jokes before; I had just never thought of them as *joke* jokes – mostly I wrote about strange things I'd seen that would have been funny if anyone had seen them. A couple of years ago, someone dropped out of a fancy talking event in a large and grand theatre in the city – the kind of old theatre that has balconies and a backstage and very ancient and loud toilets – and I was asked to replace them. I took some beta blockers my friend gave me and told a story of romantic failures. People in the audience laughed. When I told my friends how shocked I was that people laughed, they thought I was being modest. But I *wasn't* being modest – I allowed myself to become arrogant about it almost immediately. I was surprised and delighted. Could it be possible I was naturally good at something that I had taken for granted? My ego inflated like a whippet bulb. I told myself I needed to try to be more funny more often.

'I saw you speaking last night!' a girl at my admin job said the next morning. I was in a different department to this girl, so aside from small talk speculating about the multiplying bacteria in the communal microwave, we had never interacted much.

'Oh yeah?' I said, a little embarrassed but proud, too. The audience had *laughed*.

'Yeah!' she said, putting her porridge in the microwave. 'I said to my friend, "I know her!"'

I smiled, turning away and clicking on the kettle in the office kitchenette so she wouldn't see how thrilled I was. *People want to be associated with me now. Look how they tell their friends so!* Maybe my thing was jokes and – *this whole time* – everyone knew it but me. This was a turning point. 'Thank you so much!' I said, pretending to be surprised. 'I was so nervous!'

'Yeah,' she kept going, while rinsing a spoon. 'I said to my friend, "I didn't know she was funny!"' She laughed to herself, while shaking the spoon dry. The whippet bulb suddenly deflated. What felt like an annoyed porcupine started walking up and down my armpits.

'Oh,' I said. 'I guess I try to be? Sometimes.'

'Huh. Okay,' the girl said. The microwave went *bing* and she took her porridge and walked away.

Two months into the comedy show I was learning a lot, but still couldn't figure out the rhythm of how it worked. People were impressed when I told them that I was working on the telly, which felt nice. Telling them that I wasn't exactly nailing it felt unnecessary.

One particular Monday morning – a rare morning where I seemed to be able to convey the things I was thinking about with uncharacteristic clarity – I got an email from an address I had never seen before.

> *Hey Sinead,* the email started, promisingly.
>
> *I randomly came across a video of you doing a talk and almost immediately recognised you!*
>
> I knew what video it must have been: they had filmed my talk about romantic failures. My triumph.
>
> *We used to be friends and work together more than a decade ago at the burger shop. As the only two 'nerdy' people there we used to talk a lot.*
>
> *I had no idea you were so funny. I can't remember you ever saying anything funny.*
>
> *Regards,*
>
> *–LJ*

I scanned the email address. Who the fuck was 'LJ'? *Who the fuck was LJ?* I sat back in my chair, ignoring the *dings* from my work Slack and mentally running through every human I had encountered at the burger shop between 2005 and 2008.

I remembered I had once worked with a girl called BJ who I only remembered because when she started, my friend Louise whispered to me, 'Haha, funny name right?' and I whispered back, 'Yeah – like BJ Hunnicutt in *M*A*S*H*.' Louise had frowned and looked concerned. BJ had always been nice to me, and the only lengthy conversation we'd ever had was when she explained to me what the morning-after pill was while she was replacing the oil in the deep fryer. I'd been impressed by how worldly she was, though given I'd been unfamiliar with the acronym for 'blow-job', that didn't mean much. This didn't seem like the kind of email BJ would send. LJ couldn't be BJ.

I highlighted bits of LJ's email, as if this would help me comprehend it more fully.

We were *the only two nerds* at the burger shop? I remembered there being *lots* of nerds working there. There was one guy who became a mathematician. There was another guy who re-enacted whole scenes of *Family Guy*. There was a girl who had gone to a Green Day concert during the *American Idiot* years. Had LJ missed that I was friends with the older staff members? Had this person not seen the time I was handed a joint in the carpark and took a puff (I didn't inhale, but I don't think anyone noticed)? I knew I wasn't the coolest person there, but I thought I was cool-adjacent: I was friends with people who drank, had cars and knew about music. How was it possible that LJ had stored me away in their brain as the only other nerdy person in our workplace, and I had no recollection of them at all? Was it possible that LJ knew me better than I did?

Hey, do you guys remember anyone from the burger shop called LJ? I messaged Louise and our friend Ivan, who had also worked there and who was also still my friend.

Do you mean BJ? wrote Louise.

No, I wrote.

I sent them a screenshot of the email, all pretence of responding to my Slack notifications forgotten. None of us could remember who this person was. *He remembers me enough to know that I was nerdy, but doesn't remember me saying anything funny, ever?* I typed to them.

Hahaha, wrote Louise.

Hahaha! wrote Ivan.

I stopped myself from asking if they were laughing because it was a funny situation or because LJ was right.

I couldn't stop thinking about LJ for days. The group chat would update occasionally with a theory about who he could be (at this stage we all agreed it must be a man – women don't generally feel as compelled to email people they worked with ten years earlier so they can tell them they couldn't remember them ever saying anything funny).

Was he one of the twins? Louise said one morning.

Who was the weirdest person we worked with? Ivan wondered, before we all agreed that was too wide a net to cast.

They both urged me to write back and see what would happen next. I kept trying to respond to LJ, but the same question kept popping up: what did I actually *want* from him? Did I want to tell him that actually, I quite regularly got paid to be funny – like, not huge amounts, really, but currency, absolutely? Did I want to figure out why he remembered our 'nerdy' conversations much more vividly than I did? Did I want to see what happens when you email someone, *I don't remember you, sorry?* Or was I scared that if I did email back, it would give LJ the opportunity to reveal more things about me that I had deliberately tried to forget?

I never emailed back. Maybe he'll read this story. I hope he finds it funny.

Just checking, do you hate me?

Hey, it's that friend of a friend walking towards me on the street.

Haven't seen her in a while! Nice coat.

Aw jeez, I kind of hate seeing people on my lunch break. You know? It's like, this is the thirty-five minutes (an hour, I go for an hour) that I have to myself, and I want to spend it saying as little as possible to any other human being. I even avoid eye contact if I can. I know this is bad, but it's just the way I am.

I want to change but I can't change; this is the way it is, and I'm just going to have to embrace my trash personality as best I can. Don't you think I would rather be fine just eating my leftovers at the communal table and going back to my desk and just, you know, being comfortable with it? Don't you? I can't do it, it makes me itchy. I need to buy this twenty-dollar takeaway salad that's full of sultanas for some reason and sit in my 'secret park', which is just the fourth-best park in the area, and listen to a podcast and then read a book and then walk around the block for twenty minutes! So!

This girl is pretty close to me now; when we get to the 7-Eleven we'll be level. What do I say to her? Quick quick quick.

Didn't she just go on holiday? I think she did. I think I saw Bali or Thailand or South Africa or Sicily on her Instagram. Who was taking those photos of her? Okay, we'll talk about that.

Too late to duck into the 7-Eleven, isn't it.

Okay, she's approaching, here we go!

Here we go!

Here we go!

Oh!

Oh, she just ... she just walked past. She's gone. Phew! Close call! Haha.

Man, this is so good. This lunch break may have been the most silent lunch break I have ever had. No texts, no phone calls, no DMs. When I bought my twenty-dollar salad I didn't even have to say anything – the guy just knew what I was getting and he nodded, and I nodded and I tapped my card, and that was it. This is *great*. I'm a genius.

Haha.

Bit weird that she just ignored me, though? A little bit weird. Not a big deal, just a little bit weird.

Bit weird.

Okay.

Okay.

Okay, but was it an 'I didn't see you, there is a lot of sun today, I just had laser eye surgery' kind of ignore, or a 'Jesus Christ I have a giant pimple right in between my eyes like a third eye, so I cannot talk to any human I know right now' ignore, or an 'I can't talk to anyone right now' ignore, or an 'I can't talk to *you*' ignore?

It's just that she and I usually have quite good banter at a party, we follow each other on social media, she sometimes replies to my stories – is it possible I look different today? Is it possible that my hair sort of flips to the side a bit? I am growing it out. Also, it's so much straighter now. Much, much straighter hair. Used to be curly like Shirley Temple's: real ringlety, and then when I turned twenty-seven, *BLOOP*, half of it was suddenly straight and stuck out at odd angles like I had been electrocuted. I looked it up on the internet, and they said it's likely a hormonal change. So.

I just actually don't know how she didn't see me; it actually is not possible that she could have passed me on the footpath and not locked eyes with me? I think … Okay.

So I guess we're not friends.

When exactly did we become enemies, though, because I could have sworn that when we saw each other at that museum thing three or four months ago we had quite a nice conversation, and I didn't have that gnawing feeling in my stomach that I usually get after social interactions, the one that alerts me to that fact I've acted like an imbecile? I'm usually so good at identifying who hates me? Even if their reaction to me is quite neutral? It's a gift.

Was it that joke I made on Twitter about Bob Hawke? Because it wasn't meant to be a 'Ha ha Bob Hawke' joke. It was meant to be poignant.

Oh no, she's not on Twitter, I think. *Never mind.*

Maybe I should text her something, anything, and check the temperature on the situation? Facebook message her about something inane and see if she responds? Nothing like, 'Hey just checking I didn't piss you off at some point this year?' because that is too needy and bizarre; maybe just a 'This made me think of you!' and an article from *The Cut* or something. I'll figure it out later.

No! I'll message our mutual friend instead. *Do you know if I have done anything to piss this person off, was it the Bob Hawke thing, this weird thing just happened on the street?* that's more casual.

Okay, I'm doing it. I'm doing it. I'm doing it. I'm doing it. I'm doing it.

You know what, I'm not doing it. I'm letting this go. I'm trying to grow up. I'm trying to have the confidence to not take a neutral reaction as a negative reaction. This is about realising that everyone is knocking around in their own universes, all trying their best and being worried about other people's reactions, even though none of that really matters. This is about deciding that I don't need a semi-stranger being nice to me to decide that I am a good and worthy person. This is about living LIFE. This is about soothing MYSELF. This is about not building my personality around what I think is more palatable to people or changing myself so much that I don't know where people's expectations of me start and my actual personality ends.

It's okay.

Hope I don't see anyone on the tram tonight.

Some things I know about boyfriends

They appear from nowhere

In Year Eight, many people you know begin to get boyfriends. From nowhere, boyfriends are suddenly everywhere. Boyfriends are shooting up from the ground and being dropped from space wherever you look. They are large, and their voices are loud and irritating.

Some are very tall and have to bend their necks down to talk to anyone; some are short and round; some smirk every time a girl talks; some don't react when girls talk. They are discovered at school socials, train stations, parties generously attended by the nearby state school, Seventh Day Adventist community events and local football fundraising days.

'I don't really want a boyfriend,' you say to anyone who cares, because you've decided that's a cool way to be. (You wouldn't even know what to do with a boyfriend, and in any case, you sort of feel like a mistake has been made somewhere in the production line and you're actually meant to still be in Grade Six.) You try this line out at a party where there are many boys.

'Yeah, you're a good girl,' says a boy you know, one who everyone wants as their boyfriend. He looks at you kindly and gives you a gentle clap on the shoulder. You wonder if the reason so many girls like him is that he does things like gently clapping people on the shoulder.

You sit on a couch as 112's 'Dance with Me' plays on the stereo and a bunch of Year Eights in low-rise jeans clap their hands because they're sexy, and they know it. *Wait a second,* you think while watching your friends gyrate to 112. *It's really fucking bad to be a good girl, isn't it.*

There are also girlfriends

When Imogen gets a girlfriend after high school, it's exciting and you wonder if you'll have a special friendship bond with her – something you did not have with Imogen's boyfriends. You wonder if their relationship will be a lot more sophisticated and mature than heterosexual relationships. You wonder how it will change the dynamics of your social circle. You are thrilled for this new stage of Imogen's life.

It's just the same and nothing remarkable happens: girlfriends are no different to boyfriends.

They pop up in alarming places

It's your first year of uni, and you spend most of your time in tutorials trying to stop your mouth hanging limply open in horror as you realise how much smarter everyone else is. You have no idea how they know about the political history of Bolivia or have so many opinions about Virginia Woolf.

One day, you are standing in one of the university's nine libraries staring at a high bookshelf with your mouth hanging open, and a boy from your literature tutorial starts talking to you.

'Do you have a boyfriend?' he says.

'No,' you say.

'Do you want one?' he says, not looking at you.

'I don't know,' you say, then excuse yourself to go to the bathroom and stay in there for twenty minutes.

They sometimes change their mind

Your first real boyfriend is in bands and likes Death Cab for Cutie, which is the main criteria for choosing a boyfriend (though you're not entirely sure if you chose him or if you were just chosen and went along with it). One night he comes to your family home at a time when your mum is working night duty and your dad is in hospital, and he tells you he doesn't want to be your boyfriend anymore. Afterwards, Louise borrows her boyfriend's car and drives over late at night, and you sit in silence, mostly. Louise has never been properly dumped, and neither of you knows what to say. Before she leaves, she tucks you into bed like you're a little kid.

A few months later, you end up going out with someone who has exciting opinions and who you end up in screaming fights with almost every weekend. Sometimes he doesn't talk to you for days at a time and never explains why. When he eventually dumps you a year later (you dump him first, but only for show) it somehow feels like a failure. You walk around in a fog for a couple of months and cry in the work toilet most days. You watch *The Nanny* on DVD a lot.

After you have run out of *The Nanny* DVDs, you visit your friend Imogen. You sit on her couch with a blanket on your legs. She sits at the other end of the couch, and her toes rest on your leg. Her girlfriend hands you a gin and tonic and smiles at you, then leaves the room as if sensing you're about to cry and that you're not the sort of person who likes to cry in front of people. You've been too scared to drink alcohol the past few months, as if it will unplug a cork in you and all your sadness will rush out in one gush. You gingerly take a sip.

'It wasn't your fault,' says Imogen, looking at you carefully with her head propped up on her arm. 'You were trying to fix him and you couldn't fix him.'

They sometimes happen accidentally

'Do you think we could live in this house?' Andy says, pointing to a house that looks exactly like the house on either side of it.

You shrug your shoulders because you're very hot and tired and can't be bothered chatting right now, but he is still standing there with his arm stretched out pointing to the house, so you know he wants you to say yes.

'Yes,' you say.

He walks a bit further down the path, and you can tell he has found another house because he has turned around and is reaching his arm out and is pointing again. He waits until you catch up to him (you don't increase your walking pace; he doesn't lower his arm) and then he says, 'Do you think we could live in *this* house?'

The house he is pointing to has a rickety gate and an overgrown garden bursting with orange and pink and red flowers that tumble out from beneath giant lily-pad-shaped leaves. Stone steps snake up to the front door, which has a small chair next to it that you think would be good for reading. Small circular windows peek out at the lush green grass through patterned glass.

'Yes,' you say and pat him on the tummy. 'I could see us being very happy here.'

Andy quickly approaches a passing American tourist, who is holding the kind of large camera you'd take on a trek to the Andes, and holds out his phone as he asks her to take a photo. You both stand outside the house, arms around each other, and smile like you're the proud owners of a new home. Of all the houses in this life-size recreation of Hobbiton from Peter Jackson's *Lord of the Rings* trilogy – a place you've travelled to via two planes and a three-hour bus ride – this house is by far the best.

You will never remember how you actually met and became friends in the first place, when you decided to be boyfriend and girlfriend, or when you decided to move in together.

You *will* remember your first date, when he wouldn't shut up about how good *21 Jump Street* was; the time you saw an anniversary screening of *Titanic* and he held your hand when they locked the third-class people down the bottom of the ship; the time you both got chased by a single bee in New York; the time you screamed at each other at a Solange concert in New York; the time when he sweetly, accidentally, followed you to receive Communion at your grandad's funeral even though he wasn't Catholic, and it made your cousins laugh and cheered them up for a while (he crossed his hands on his chest and got a blessing instead); the time when you hid under a blanket because you were so embarrassed about something, and instead of pulling the blanket off you, he put his head under the blanket, too, and said, 'HELLOOO!' in a Mrs Doubtfire voice.

One day you realise you've been going out for almost nine years and it makes you laugh so much you cry. 'Why are you laughing?' says Andy, who also starts laughing. You decide to be his girlfriend forever.

4

The soul

'A journey of a thousand miles begins with a single step, but make sure you're stepping at the same pace as everyone else. Like, that's extremely important.'

—*JRR Tolkien*

Weekend

About once a week, unless it has been one of those weeks where I am occupied with nameless dread, I think about a particular episode of *The Oprah Winfrey Show* that aired in 1997. This episode was promoting the movie *The First Wives Club* and featured the stars Goldie Hawn, Bette Midler and Diane Keaton gabbing with Oprah about ageing, female empowerment and what it's like to have so much money that you could dive into a pool of it like Scrooge McDuck.

The three women look very expensive. They also look like they're experiencing completely different weather conditions. Goldie is wearing a probably-cashmere black skivvy and tight black pants with sandals. Bette is wearing a lime-green two-piece suit with a short skirt. Diane is wearing a pinstriped shirt, a bow tie, a heavy leather trench coat and a green bowler hat.

There's a moment in this episode that has taken residence in a corner of my brain. It happens early on: Goldie, Bette and

Oprah have just finished talking about how they deal with ageing ('If you don't keep yourself in shape, you get osteoporosis,' – Midler) when Keaton adds, 'Basically, I think getting older means that you're closer to death.'

The other women try to recover from this moment of nihilism by discussing how it's important to live your life with 'no regrets' and 'no loose ends', and that's the only way to make your peace with death (by the way, this is only three minutes into the episode; it would take Ellen at least twenty minutes to get her guests to discuss their own mortality).

Oprah talks about why it is important to stimulate joy in yourself. Midler finds joy in dancing. Hawn finds joy in existing. 'What are you doing to have fun?' Oprah asks Keaton, who is smirking at the other women.

'I like watching television,' she says.

Midler laughs so much that she tips to the side of her chair (towards Hawn, a happy person) and starts kicking out one of her legs in time with her cackles.

'You do!?' says Oprah, incredulous.

'I do,' says Keaton. 'And I'm not ashamed, either.'

Keaton explains that when you've been busy working all day it's quite nice to go home and watch some television. The other three women continue to laugh in a pitying way, as if watching a puppy fall into a puddle, lose its balance, and then fall into a puddle again.

I have never related to someone more. I would like to be the sort of person who finds joy in exercise, like Midler, or in a research project about happiness, like Hawn, or whatever Oprah does on the weekend. (Gardening? Harvesting clones?) These activities seem to be indicative of good character. They're wholesome. They're the kind of thing you're meant to want to do. But really, I am happiest when I am at home, without interruption, watching television. And not important prestige television about drug dealers and complicated men and robots dressed as cowboys, but unimportant television that I have already seen a thousand times before. I would probably horrify Oprah, too.

Keaton is happy when she's watching television, which is judged to be a concerning type of happy. Watching lots of TV is often seen as a sign of laziness – particularly if you're watching *Downton Abbey* again and again for no other reason than you quite like it. When Keaton says in justification that there's just 'so many channels!' to watch, I feel it in my (slovenly) bones. For me, being home alone and rewatching a film or series is the equivalent of a scented candle, a week of meditation, a jasmine-oil diffuser and two valium. But I know that divulging this makes me seem like a sad and maybe pathetic person whom the Bette Midlers and Goldie Hawns of the world would feel sympathy for (presumably before taking a run in the park and spending the afternoon planting fennel).

When I tell you about the kind of things that I crave watching when I am alone, you will feel sorry for me. Worse than when I watch things I have seen a thousand times (not just *Downton*, but *Gilmore Girls*, *The O.C.*, *Frasier*, *The Crown*,

Friends, Dawson's Creek, Skins …) is when I watch shows that I know are both intellectually and emotionally bad for me. Before you ask, this isn't an excuse to rail on reality television, which to my mind can be educational (*Selling Sunset*, for instance, made me realise that the richer you are, the uglier you want your house to be). When I tell you this, you're going to look at me (or this page) in the same way that Bette Midler and Goldie Hawn looked at Diane Keaton, which is to say you'll be almost frightened to be associated with me. My confession is that on a Friday night, while you are having after-work drinks and seeing bands, I often like to stay at home alone, horizontal on the couch, and watch *This is Us* while crying hysterically.

This is Us is a truly terrible show, really quite awful, which you can probably guess from the title because it doesn't even try to be anything other than what it is. It is about triplets called Kevin, Kate and Randall, and it jumps back and forth to different tragic moments in their lives. Randall is adopted, which is frequently a topic of sombre conversation. Their mother is Mandy Moore, who sometimes plays a 25-year-old version of herself, then puts on glasses and plays a 65-year-old version of herself. Their dad is played by the guy who played Jess in *Gilmore Girls*, and we are told immediately through flashback that he is dead, but the show doesn't explain how he dies for about forty episodes, so every scene he is in you're just sort of waiting for him to die. The show contains multiple timelines in every episode, showing different horrible things that have happened at different stages of the triplets' lives.

This is to say that *This is Us* is the sort of television show that was created with the express purpose of making you cry during every single episode. It doesn't even matter what the episode is about. It could be about Randall getting a promotion, or Kevin working on a movie with Sylvester Stallone, or Kate auditioning to be a singer in a band – it doesn't matter, because it will somehow figure out how to make you cry. Randall will inevitably have a psychotic break at work, Kevin will eventually hurt his leg in front of Sly Stallone and get addicted to painkillers, Kate will make herself vulnerable only to get rejected. And this happens in *every episode*.

I don't believe in guilty pleasures as a concept, but if I did I would classify *This is Us* as one, because of the way I find myself behaving when I am caught watching it. If I hear my boyfriend come home while I am watching *This is Us*, I turn it off quickly and try to hide the evidence, as if I have been caught cheating or smoking pot in my bedroom. If he asks, 'What are you watching, babe?' I say, 'Nothing.' If he questions me any more than that, I suddenly become furious. I wonder if he thinks I try to watch porn every time he leaves the house. I kind of hope so, as that is less embarrassing.

Having recently run out of traumatic episodes of *This is Us*, I started watching *13 Reasons Why*, which is even more deplorable and is so deplorable, in fact, that the start of each season contains a PSA about seeking help for emotional distress generally, but also in relation to how the show makes you feel. At the end of each episode there's a special hotline and website you can visit. It is a show about a group of teenagers who endure the following: sexual assault, physical abuse, drug abuse, bullying, body-shaming, self-harm, isolation, false imprisonment, racism, sexism, homophobia, attempted murder, suicide, and one of them even has their family deported to Puerto Rico. *Maybe I should watch an episode of* Deadwood, I think to myself every time I fire up a new episode. *Maybe I should finally try* The Newsroom. But these shows would be too artistic, and these nights are not for art. These nights aren't about being productive. These nights are for doing nothing.

The problem is that there is a lot of shame around doing nothing. People get mad when you like doing nothing. For many, weekends need to be production factories that include a longer to-do list than the average workday. There are workouts and brunches and runs to the market and visits to the dry cleaner and picnics and football and art galleries and dinners and drinks and Skype calls and spring cleaning and wardrobe cleanouts and yoga. If you don't tick off everything on the list, you've wasted your weekend. And if you've dared to do nothing, you risk looking pathetic on Monday morning when someone asks you what you did on the weekend. You mutter 'watched TV' apologetically; they look at you in pity and then shuffle off to talk to someone who at least went on a hike. You have failed at the concept of a weekend.

I once read an article in *1843* magazine called 'The way out of burnout' in which psychoanalyst Josh Cohen says people who suffer burnout at work often have a hard time with the concept of relaxing on the weekend. When they take time off from their demanding jobs, they automatically start filling up their free time with a schedule of 'relaxing tasks' because the idea of being unproductive makes them feel lazy. This internalised idea that one's worth is tied to one's achievement means that even in their time off, victims of burnout can't feel truly calm. They can't watch *This is Us*, because *This is Us* isn't furthering them emotionally or intellectually or socially and thus holds no value.

But what if we actively *started doing things that are bad for us*? Maybe this is wrong. Maybe the entire self-care movement is against me. But also! Maybe this is part of resisting the great capitalist energy that is trying to turn us into robots whose every impulse is tied to efficiency and whose value is tied to their output? Maybe we need to spend some time indulging in dumb shit. Maybe I am trying to intellectualise my desire to watch a show about the various emotional traumas inflicted upon three attractive siblings over the course of thirty years. Too bad: I'm writing this story and I can't hear you saying that I'm wrong!

Of course, some people love to be extremely busy. But if, for other people, the best way to relax is to do nothing, then the idea of finding joy in simply watching TV shouldn't seem so tragic. In that *Oprah* episode from 1997, after Keaton has divulged on television that she likes watching television, Oprah collects herself and asks, 'Where is that on the fun meter for you?'

Keaton replies with a smile: 'Ten, baby!' and Oprah makes the sounds 'OH HO HO!' which is close enough to the sound of a laugh to be polite.

Maybe one day Keaton and I will be able to reveal our relaxation techniques without fear of mockery. Until then, I will watch TV on Friday night, by myself, in peace. If the mood takes me, I might put on *The First Wives Club*.

The good host

Have you ever had that thing.

Where you invite people over.

(Which is a thing in itself.)

And you know you need to have music playing when they come in, otherwise it just looks like you've been sitting in silence with your hands folded in your lap waiting for them to arrive, which, you know.

Is a thing that murderers do.

So you need to choose music that you could conceivably just be playing for yourself, rather than obviously performative music for visitors.

(Usually people choose David Bowie or Fleetwood Mac, because it shows that you're interesting but not interesting enough to prompt any follow-up questions, which would naturally be a disaster.)

(You know, one of those non-offensive bands you can play

in an office without the threat of anyone actually finding out anything about you.)

(If you pick dance music you worry that it may look quite desperate, like you need the night to be SUPER EPIC or that you think that they are the sort of people who can only socialise in a 'shots, shots, shots!' way.)

And then your guests arrive and you have to pretend you're just the sort of person who always has wine in the fridge and music playing casually and clean glasses in the cupboard and heaps of toilet paper? Maybe you've even lit the 'special candle'?

It's weird is all I'm saying.

Out with the old

My boyfriend and I are on the street and we are screaming at each other.

Well, this is only half the truth. Andy doesn't scream at me, really. He hates confrontation and is more likely to make a scowling noise like 'cacha-urgh!', as though he's a kindly grandfather or local parish priest who is frustrated but trying not to swear in front of you. I am the one doing most of the screaming. The reason I am screaming is because he has put my television on the nature strip for hard rubbish and I think this is not only a nonsensical decision, but a total violation of my civil liberties.

'Why would you do this?!' I scream with the fury of betrayal, my arms flailing about like a marionette's. An alarmed child whizzes by us on his scooter.

'Because it was broken?' he says, before looking away and saying 'cacha-urgh!' to no one.

The most annoying thing about all this is that I know he's right. We don't need that TV anymore. The TV is old. It will sometimes turn off for no good reason. It sometimes won't even turn on for no good reason, only to do so with a jolt several hours later. Whenever that happens, I think to myself, *Poltergeist?* but I know it's more likely that the TV is just suffering a severe internal haemorrhage. Occasionally we'll be watching something and purple squiggles will appear across the screen like a giant toddler is taking to it with a texta. It is the most obstinate appliance I own. But my parents gave me this TV ten years ago! My hard-working parents, who have withstood so much, gifted this to me! How could I insult them like this by abandoning it? It's part of the family.

Andy and I have had this confrontation before. Before my broken TV, it was a cracked baking dish and an old, stained saucepan. Before that, it was our old, gross pillows that felt like trying to sleep on an empty sack of flour, as if we were wayward youths riding the rails in the 1920s. I even know what the next one will be, because Andy has hinted at it: our creaky bed that I bought from IKEA seven years ago, which sags on one side because the wooden slats (which, to be fair, are held together by elastic and staples) always slip out.

The problem is, I can't throw stuff away. Even writing the phrase 'throw stuff away' makes my heart break a little bit. I am almost crying right now imagining throwing anything away. Every time I try to get rid of an ill-fitting cardigan, old CD or broken toiletry bag, I experience the same internal struggle. *What if the house burns down and my clothes are gone and the only thing that survives is this old cardigan?* I wonder. *What if this CD was bought with a voucher I once received from my grandparents, who are gone now?* I think sadly. *What If I need to flee during the night and the only thing I have to hold my face creams in is this pouch?* I wonder, while trying to move the broken zipper on the stained toiletry bag.

Because of this logic, I have desk drawers, cupboards, bookcases and storage bags stuffed with notes, old toys, CDs, Christmas cards, ill-fitting jackets, unused eyeshadow palettes, old diaries, broken torches, and gifted shower-gel packs. I wouldn't call myself a hoarder because I haven't got towering piles of newspapers placed around the house (though, when I didn't see my parents for six months during the COVID-19 lockdown, I did hold on to one newspaper my dad had left on his last visit because I couldn't bring myself to throw it out). I preserve sentiment like a curator at a museum. There are pockets of melodramatic emotion stuffed all around my house.

The attachment to inanimate objects becomes more pronounced when I'm moving house and need to sort through my useless possessions. Suddenly odd socks or broken lamps are imbued not only with personal histories, but with personalities. As they sit in my hand anticipating the moment they are to be discarded, they beg me, *Sinéad, please do not throw me out, please, my friend.* The beating of their tiny hearts echoes in the room and syncs up with my own. Suddenly I am some sort of mad king sending my wives to the executioner when the problem actually lies with me. *Does this sock deserve this?* I think. *Won't it be lonely if I throw it out?* I am a genius at inventing *Velveteen Rabbit*-esque narratives around possessions I have forgotten I even have.

I often think about items I have owned that will never be able to come home again, like they are my soldier sweethearts stranded on the beaches of Dunkirk. When my first boyfriend and I broke up, I was so wretched that I couldn't even bring myself to get the stuff that I left at his house (which included my Laura Palmer T-shirt, a *Do the Right Thing* T-shirt and a DVD copy of *La Haine*). I had only bumped into him at uni once since the breakup, and the encounter had been so taxing and full of anguished tears (his, not mine – that seems important to mention) that I couldn't imagine going through another dramatic untangling.

'Did you loan him any money?' one of my classmates asked later in a tutorial, as I explained the encounter and asked advice on how to rescue my poor possessions.

'I guess so,' I said, unable to explain that the financial aspect wasn't really the concern.

'I never feel bad for chicks who loan guys money,' he said, shaking his head.

I did really like those T-shirts, and *La Haine* really is a very good movie, but that's sort of beside the point. I am not a very greedy person, and, though I like to be surrounded by nice things, it's not absolutely vital to my happiness to have candles and precious ceramics and endless *things* around me at all times. I once read that people who have experienced any sort of instability in their lives have a hard time throwing stuff away, because there's always a little voice at the back of their heads warning them that fortunes change easily and their livelihoods can dissolve quickly. You train yourself to always be a little bit on edge just in case you need to sling your possessions over your back and make a move, which means the fear of throwing something out only to not be able to replace it floats over every minor decision. Throwing away a broken TV may seem reasonable, but it's hard to soothe yourself when your automatic thought is, *But what if I never own a TV ever again?* (Or, even more dramatically, *What if my parents disappear tomorrow and this is the last reminder I have of them?*) It's just a tricky impulse to tame.

For the last couple of years, I've been able to put aside a little money in each pay cycle, and I actually have savings. It's not a huge amount, but it's an amount I'm proud of. I'm trying to make myself more comfortable with the idea that if something really bad happens and I lose vital possessions or need to move quickly, I will be able to bail myself out – financially, anyway. Unless I decide to become a mysterious vagabond and blow it all on a travelling caravan, which I always like to keep as an option.

I give in and let go of the TV only when Andy's dad gives us his old one, which is so heavy that it takes the two of them to lift it into our apartment – and only with frequent breaks of putting it down and panting. It's one of those TVs that is probably designed for people who live in big lofts or converted churches with high ceilings. If you live in a normal apartment it appears to take up roughly the space of a Jackson Pollock painting, and even if you push the couch to the very furthest corner of your living room, watching it still feels like hurtling your eyeballs into space.

'This TV is great!' Andy says. Months later he admits that even he feels 'a little bit woozy' when scrolling through the Netflix menu.

The new–old TV is so large and weighty that we need to get a new, larger table to support its chunky mass. I find a wooden slab on Facebook Marketplace for $35 and the two young women who are selling it offer to drive it to our place.

'I'm sort of sad to give this up,' one of the women says when they pull up with the table, while the other woman frowns. I give the sadder woman an understanding nod.

'We'll take good care of it,' I say, with a smile.

The anatomy of a good, grown-up apartment

A plant

Plants! I need plants! I'm worried about my plants! I need to water my plants! Please stay at my house this weekend and water my plants!

Plants are the apartment status symbols of the 20th century. It is not enough to be able to keep yourself alive, you must prove that you can also keep something constantly growing and needing in your home. You should have a few plants in your living room, with leaves the size of hands, but having some in your bathroom is also advised because it increases the life-and-death drama of what is already the most dramatic room in the house. Hanging plants are the best ones because they make it seem as if you have defied gravity; that's how in control of your house you are.

Your plants should be the kind of plants that can survive bitter winters and scorching summers. But maybe even we humans won't survive what the future will bring! Haha.

A hand-held grater to shave delicate slices of parmesan

It's a scientific fact that if you, in front of a guest of any sexual orientation, grab a great hunk of parmesan and hold it over a bowl of pasta and then proceed to grate delicate little shavings of parmesan on top of the pasta, rhythmically moving the hunk back and forth so the cheese falls romantically like snow on a mountain-top, that guest will fall in love immediately and want to have sex with you. I don't know why. It just happens.

(No vegans.)

A candle

Open flames make guests feel relaxed, and candles make them feel extra relaxed because the nice ones often cost a lot of money and people genuinely feel safer when they're in proximity to money. The best thing to do is to burn a candle fifteen minutes before your guests arrive, and then when they arrive at the designated time, still have that faux, slightly surprised, 'Oh, you're here!' thing, even though you all agreed on the time and the candle is already burning.

The best candle types are the ones that sound like they could be Biblical villains: 'Santal', 'Baies', 'Bibliothèque' etc.

An artisanal ceramic plate

You need to have a handmade ceramic plate that is meant for keys, but seems kind of too nice for keys, so you just put hair ties and spare buttons on there, which is certainly not what the artist intended.

A drink cart

It's important for others to think that you're the kind of person who comes home after work and mixes themselves a single Negroni or Aperol Sour or other drink that makes your tongue want to curl back into your throat. This is what successful people do. Successful people drink exactly one drink a night. They do this while watching the nightly news or sitting in an armchair and looking wistfully out the window. Maybe they're thinking of what their life might have been. Maybe they're thinking of that girl they liked in first-year uni and should have married. Maybe they're thinking about how on Christmas Eve last year they Facebook messaged the girl like, *Hey … hope you're well!* and the girl saw the message and said nothing, so they messaged back a few days later, *Sorry! That wasn't for you. Hope you're well anyway!* and the girl saw it *again* and didn't reply, and then they deleted their Facebook and deleted their Instagram and deleted their Twitter and told everyone at work that they were doing a 'digital detox', which was met with many congratulations.

Just get a lot of tall bottles of red liquid, is what I'm saying.

A cream-coloured rug with boobs drawn on it

Prove that you're fun!

A piece of art that is sort of mocking you

Having art in your house is the easiest way to communicate that you are a grown-up who has figured this whole thing out, without showing guests payslips to prove that you make regular super payments.

There are two kinds of art that will make your guests feel comfortable, as they will undoubtedly have similar art in their own homes. These types are a) pastel splodges and b) art that seems to be making fun of you and all of your possessions. This art could be a black-and-white sketch that includes a caption like, *My home is crap!* or maybe a pop-art face crying, with a speech bubble that says, *Is this it?* or a collage of a dog in space with *I AM TRYING MY BEST, THAT IS ALL I CAN DO* written in cursive.

This art will make you look self-deprecating and humble about how nice your house is. All of your art should make your guests feel compelled to ask if you're okay.

Books

Books! People need to see that you have books! It doesn't matter what you actually read, and to be honest, it's almost better not to put those books on display. Who wants to talk to people about something they're *reading*? Who wants to pretend to care about other people's *opinions*? Exactly.

Here are a list of books you should stack in your bookshelf, without fear that one of your guests will ask you about them because they haven't read them either: *A Moveable Feast*, *War and Peace*, *An Inconvenient Truth*, *Crime and Punishment*, *Freedom* (I actually have read that one, but forgot what happened even when I was actually reading it), *The Happiness Trap*, anything by Philip Roth and *The Road*.

A cashmere throw

All the houses worth visiting have a cashmere throw lying on the couch. The throw should be draped on the couch in such a way that it looks like the wind carried it there. This cashmere throw will have cost far too much to plop on your lap while eating spaghetti or to let a dog sit on. You should always wash your hands before touching it. You shouldn't shout in its presence. During thunderstorms, you should pat it comfortingly to let it know that it has found safety here. You should stop in the doorway and ask its permission whenever you want to enter the living room.

A wooden dining table

'This will be great for when we have people over!' you'll say, before never inviting people over to your house and eating all your meals over the coffee table.

Soap made with Australian native plants

If you have any soap in your house that is French-vanilla- or linen-scented, your guests will probably vomit at the first sniff of it and leave, because those soap flavours aren't chic anymore. The only soap flavours that you are allowed to have are soaps that smell like camping. If your soap doesn't smell like tea-tree or eucalyptus or lemon myrtle or wattle or gum nuts, then you are a Luddite and a fraud and probably don't even use soap. You probably slop in the mud like a common swine. You probably lick your hands clean like a street cat. You probably condition your hair with handfuls of lard.

The only soap that matters is the kind that might give you a rash.

A record player

Now that CDs are dead, it's more difficult to display your identity and taste in an incidental-looking but deeply deliberate way. This is where a record player comes in. A record player is eccentric. A record player is considered. A record player is so impressive and yet useless that its main value will lie in people approaching it and saying, 'Oh, a record player!' and you will say, 'Yes,' and that's where the conversation will end. Records are very expensive, so just cut some black cardboard circles and put them into record sleeves. No one will ask to listen to them anyway.

A spare room

A place for the old Christmas cards and the clothes horse and your exercise bike and the bread maker and the desk you don't use and the old typewriter you don't use and your hopes and dreams and broken phones.

Cool job

I used to work in a very pristine office. The walls were made of white bricks and the ground was made of polished wooden floorboards. Huge windows invited the afternoon sun to rush in, while the air conditioner disavowed the sun by perpetually keeping us at 23 degrees Celsius all year round. We enjoyed the sun in theory only. The tables were off-white, and sitting on the tables were silver screens and minimal personal artefacts. There were many plants, and the plants were tasteful. Cheese platters appeared on Fridays. And every few months, the entire office smelled like human shit.

I think when I started the job someone did mention to me that every few months the office would smell like human shit, but I thought it was some sort of joke about the state of the industry, so laughed and then went back to trying to memorise the door code. No one had quite been able to properly explain why this happened. Or maybe they had tried to explain it, but it only really came up while the smell was happening, at which point it was impossible to stay in the office for more than a ten-minute stretch.

For most of the year, this office was the kind of office that appears on job-recruitment websites. It was clean and well-lit and minimalist and included thoughtful details like coat racks and a coffee machine. It was a real *grown-up* office – which was kind of appealing, given how many of the offices I had worked in had involved the rattle of pinball machines and ping-pong balls whizzing past my head. Those offices looked fun but were almost never fun. A ping-pong table wouldn't have lasted two seconds here.

The office usually didn't smell like anything, which is an attribute that you don't consider valuable until it's gone. But for a few days every year – not even the full day, usually just until lunchtime – this strange phenomenon occurred. The blame rested squarely on the restaurant above the office, which, every now and then, needed a big truck to come and drain an excess of *something* (some people said it was sewage, some people said it was used cooking oil – though I worked in hospo for years and never smelled any oil like that) and then drove off to carry it … somewhere? This process took several hours. It was unclear why this happened, but happen it did.

'Oh no, it's the poo truck,' people would say as they entered the office, pinching their noses so the poo molecules couldn't get in. Some people stayed at their desks and diligently tried to work as if nothing at all was happening, as if breathing in poo air was just a normal part of their workday. Other people started gagging immediately and declared they were working from home. Some retreated to nearby cafes and took up valuable table real estate while only ordering one filter coffee over three hours.

'I once worked at a place where I dealt with a similar gross thing,' I once told a table of new colleagues while we were enjoying the cafe's faeces-free air. 'Once, when I was working at Jay Jays, someone went to the changing room and did a poo in a T-shirt, then put that T-shirt back onto a giant pile of T-shirts that were on sale.'

'Oh my god!' one of the girls said, covering her mouth.

'I know,' I said, emboldened. 'One of the customers found it. Pretty gross, huh?'

The table was quiet. I had gone too far. We launched into our WIP as if no one was thinking about being a customer who picked up a T-shirt with poo in it. It really was a grown-up workplace.

(The fantasy of) my brilliant career

When you are little, before the world has had its way with you, you sometimes think about what the future will bring. As an adult, I hate thinking about the future; it's as if the future is a delicate balloon full of boiling water, and if I handle it and fidget with it and focus on it too much it will burst, sending boiling water cascading over my hands. But when I was little, I didn't attach such unsettling metaphors to pondering what lay ahead.

I know now that many kids think about the domestic situation that might await them, a sort of gold-tinged vision of themselves married and with a kid. Maybe they think of their wedding day. Maybe they think of homemade birthday cakes in light-filled dining rooms. I never dreamed of any of this; instead, I spent a lot of time thinking about what job I wanted to do. It's not because I'm a perfect feminist – I spent far too much time playing out 'prince rescues the princess' Barbie scenarios to ever be called that – but rather that I wanted to seem impressive. I wanted people to look at me in admiration. I wanted to *matter*.

The older you get and the longer you work, the more you realise that the fantasy doesn't always match up to the reality. It's like sipping a beer for the first time and being so excited, then thinking, *Why does this taste like used bathwater from the tub of a thousand-year-old man?*

Pursuing a career is a game of managing expectations, is what I'm saying.

The *To Kill a Mockingbird* stage

It is impossible to read the book *To Kill a Mockingbird* and not conclude that law is the only worthwhile profession. It doesn't matter what age you are when you read this book for the first time, but it helps if you are between ten and fourteen. I do not know how you can read *To Kill a Mockingbird* and not decide that you want to be a lawyer. I genuinely don't. I'm not sure how you're able to read that whole book and only come away from it saying, 'Oh, that was a good book, just like everyone says,' or, 'Okay, Boo Radley has taught me that just because people are different doesn't mean they're to be feared,' or 'White people sure have a tendency to prioritise their comfort over almost anything else.' Those are good things to take away from it, I don't dispute that. But I'm not entirely sure why you would bother pursuing any other career after you've finished reading it.

You read *To Kill a Mockingbird*, and you spend the next two or three years telling everyone who will listen that you're going to be a lawyer, 'just like Atticus'. You know that you don't have a cool enough name to be a lawyer, but you could always change that later on. You can so clearly picture yourself conjuring an aura of quiet dignity and heroically disregarding the personal cost of always doing the right thing. You scour newspapers for injustices that you can pontificate about at the dinner table, to prove to your family how noble you are. In your fantasies, you stand up for people without voices and are praised for your moral courage by admirers who witness your good deeds. It doesn't occur to you that good deeds can exist without being witnessed by admirers. You pray that you will one day need spectacles, so you can wearily take them off and clean them on your waistcoat while sighing deeply about injustice.

You know that being a lawyer requires a lot of studying and that it often takes you a very long time to understand abstract concepts or to stop yourself zoning out within two minutes of embarking on an intellectual activity you're not immediately good at. But you figure that those are problems for later on.

(In Year Nine, when my English teacher, Mrs Val, realised that I had already read *To Kill a Mockingbird*, she assigned me another book to read while the rest of my class read Harper Lee. At first she suggested *Angela's Ashes*, and my dad said no, which I found thrilling. Her next choice was *Cat's Eye* by Margaret Atwood. I didn't understand a single word of it. Mrs Val was disappointed.)

The prime-minister stage

Somewhere around the time you realise that being a lawyer often has less to do with fighting injustice in the Deep South and more to do with wearing suits, passing tests and reading real-estate contracts, you decide that you can probably fight injustice in another way and that this career isn't big enough for your gaping ambition.

'I'm going to be the prime minister,' you say to Mrs Val, while she is driving you to a debating competition.

She laughs. 'Good idea!' she says.

'The first *female* prime minister,' you clarify, so she can appreciate how momentous your decision to be prime minister really is. Mrs Val nods, keeping her eyes on the road.

In early high school you are quite good at speaking in public (something that you have since lost in the slow march of time). Prime minister is a natural fit. Anyone can stand and talk in a courtroom – you've thought about it and decided that must be quite easy – but they don't let that many people speak in parliament. What an inspiration you will be to the young women of Australia! Being the first woman in charge is a vital part of this plan, as it makes it harder, and things that are hard are the only things worth achieving.

'You should be on the radio!' says your aunty Grainne, laughing, when you explain your ambitions to your family that Christmas.

'Thanks!' you say, not realising that it isn't exactly a compliment.

Many years later, when you tell Grainne that you're taking a break from media and working in an advertising agency for a while, she says, 'Oh, no. Advertising?' You barely last at that job for a year. Aunty Grainne is good at keeping you grounded.

You forget all about this plan to be the first female prime minister, until you go with your family to a St Patrick's Day party fifteen years later. The party is full of people your dad knew from working in construction, men who were regular fixtures of your early teenage years.

'Ahhh, do you remember when all you cared about was being prime minister?' says a man named John, after challenging you as to why you aren't married. 'Remember when you made us take you to Canberra?'

'Haha,' you say, sort of wishing that he would go back to hypothesising as to why no one has asked you to marry them yet.

'So, what are you doing now?' says John.

'Um … branded content?' you say, waiting to see if this registers.

'What?' John says.

'I edit branded content – like articles, but for brands,' you say. John nods and goes back to talking to your dad. Your sister grimaces at you and shrugs sympathetically.

The *Almost Famous* stage

The summer that *Almost Famous* comes out on DVD, you watch it once a day every day for the entire school holidays. You can't recall where you got the money to rent it from DeeJay's Video, but presumably it involved a search of couch cushions and car floors. You want to be like William Miller and follow Stillwater around the country in 1973, even though nothing about that was remotely possible. You want an older critic like Lester Bangs to take you under his wing and explain to you how to listen for the 'vast scenic bridges and angelic choirs in your head' and to have opportunities to say things like 'vast scenic bridges and angelic choirs in your head'. You want to be part of something massive, filled with emotions that cannot be contained. You read books by Lester Bangs before realising that you actually want to be like Philip Seymour Hoffman as Lester Bangs. You buy a 1979 copy of *Rolling Stone* with The Blues Brothers on the cover. You put a canvas portrait of Hunter S Thompson up on your bedroom wall like you're a boy undertaking an arts degree. You buy the *Forrest Gump* soundtrack to learn about classic rock. You read interviews written by Cameron Crowe. You listen to so much Simon & Garfunkel.

'Sinéad, you're not cool enough to work at *Rolling Stone*,' says your friend Whitney, a girl who is captain of many sports teams and later goes on to be a reporter on one of those programs where they chase real-estate frauds outside of courthouses. You spend the next five or six years doing the cultural homework you think is necessary to get a job at *Rolling Stone*. You get a job at a fast-food chicken shop and spend all your money on CDs and magazines. You barely speak to anyone at school about music, because you assume they won't understand it as well as you do (snobbery is an important part of all this; you're learning that quickly).

'Don't you want to be a lawyer, though?' says your dad hopefully.

You don't want to let him down by explaining that you're not actually as smart as he thinks you are, so you just say, 'No!' as if that is the weirdest and funniest narc thing anyone has ever suggested.

When you grow up, for the very first time, the job that you fantasised about is the job that you're actually *doing*. You can't fathom that people are actually paying you for your thoughts about music. Sure, you're not being sent across America for a two-thousand-word cover story, but it still feels good.

You write album reviews for street-press magazines that no one reads; you write live blog posts about Kanye West crashing the stage at the VMAs that no one reads; you interview Kele from Bloc Party and he says, 'Think of a better question,' because he mishears what you've said; you interview Carrie Brownstein and cry afterwards because you think you've fucked it; Josh Schwartz tweets that you 'made his day' after you write about 'Music from The O.C.'; one of the best rock critics on the planet tells you 'analysing Drake is your superpower' and you believe her; you interview Kylie Minogue and don't mention that you regularly watch her performance at the closing ceremony of the 2000 Olympics – it's all fantastic, and you write thinkpieces for *Pitchfork* that people read and it terrifies you. Men start appearing in your DMs asking for email addresses of American editors. You get a bit bored of justifying why you're qualified to write about music. You feel grateful that you've had this rarefied opportunity, but it does occur to you that making your hobby your job does sort of make your leisure time feel like homework. You stop listening to new music for a while and go back to listening to the bloghouse bands from 2007 that you liked when you were eighteen. It helps you to remember why you like music.

The internship stage

You go to uni and forget to learn any life skills, so then you go to another uni and they set you up with an internship at one of the biggest media companies in Australia. Several of the teachers at the uni have laughed when you say you want to be a film critic (a side ambition to wanting to be a music critic) because there are only two or three full-time film-critic jobs in Australia and they're all occupied by men in their forties who won't retire for another two decades at least. You're thrilled to hear that this is a profession in which people can accrue enough money to retire one day.

'Lifestyle' writing is your only possible hope to earn a living from writing, but even then you're told that if you don't do hard news at a regional paper for at least two years after graduating, you won't even deserve to write captions in spring racing print features.

You buy a black skirt from Target and black tights from the supermarket and ask for black boots for your birthday so you can pretend to be a grown-up during the two-week internship that your uni has set up at the street press arm of a large media company. You're terrified of having to interview people on the phone in an open-plan office, where everyone can hear you ask stupid questions. The journalists around you seem so adult, but you later realise that they were all seven to eight years older than you at most. You eat lunch by yourself because you're too scared to talk to anyone, and you suddenly become aware of how loud your steps are in the office. A couple of days after your internship finishes, the editor calls you and says he'd like you to come in and help out a few days a week, indefinitely. You're sad to leave your job at Borders, but not overly sad given you've recently been advised that the company will likely go 'into administration', which you don't exactly understand but are sure is not positive.

You decide you can just wear your normal clothes to the media job. You get described as 'quirky' by women who wear high heels. In the first month of you working there full-time (as a casual worker – you never get an actual contract) it is announced that three hundred people across the company will be losing their jobs. A whole floor of the building is left completely deserted, the desks littered with abandoned pens and staplers, and the office chairs at odd angles. It looks like a place that people were made to leave very quickly, which reminds you of a zombie apocalypse movie.

That same month, you see Prime Minister Julia Gillard in the elevator. She doesn't look very happy. You think of saying 'good job!' to cheer her up, but instead you give her a thumbs up and then immediately want to die.

The actually getting a job you want stage

Oh, the thrill of writing something and seeing it in print! Oh, the thrill of writing something and seeing it immediately appear online!

Oh, the thrill of people *reading* what I have *written* and finding something in there that they like and relate to; the joy! Oh, the thrill of endless money being available for this youth media website, oh no you have been made redundant, oh wait it's okay, here is another job!

Oh, the thrill of someone in your family saying, 'Hey, I read that thing you wrote about the Beastie Boys,' and other people in your family saying, 'Cool, link me to that'! Oh, the thrill of being asked to edit people's work and being told that, though they can't pay you more than a staff-writer salary, you are still an integral part of this youth media brand!

Oh, the thrill of going freelance and just writing and writing and invoicing and pitching and writing and writing and writing –

Oh no, *Game of Thrones* is over, what do I write about now?

The getting a job that isn't your passion but doesn't keep you awake at night stage

Wait, so you can actually just go to an office, do a job and then go home and not think about it that much? If you stop checking your email after 6pm, it's not an indication that you're irresponsible and lazy? Working for money and leave is okay? A job can just be a job and not the measure of your worth and ambition? You don't have to do it forever, it's just something you get paid to do?

Seems suspicious.

The deciding capitalism is the enemy AKA have I run out of ambition or am I just a bit sleepy? stage

Probably a bit of both.

How to start a new job during a pandemic

'Obviously, this is a really strange time,' said a lady named Alana.

Alana had called me the week before my first day at my new job, which was a type of job I had never tried to do before. 'It's so strange!' I said to her, agreeing that this whole thing was quite strange. It felt as though I had been agreeing with people on the phone (it was so strange!) for three weeks. Everyone who had been able to had started working at home almost a month ago, and no one was very sure about when that would end but thought that it should probably end soon. Offices all over the city had been abandoned in haste: dirty coffee cups were left on counters, whiteboards were littered with now irrelevant brainstorms from the first week of March and keyboards lay unused on desks. Presumably, rats were roaming freely through kitchenettes. Maybe the rats were using the keyboards. Maybe they were writing excellent rat novels in rat language we couldn't even identify. The adrenaline of the first weeks had worn off and now we were in the exhaustion phase. By April everyone was saying to each other, 'I mean, who knows how long it will last? What do you think?' and then someone else would say, 'It's just so hard to tell!' and every few days, you would swap parts and start all over again. It really was so strange.

I knew that all my work at this new job would take place over Slack chats, Google Docs and Zoom calls, but I still wasn't sure what the nature of this work would be – how would my days be structured? Who would I be reporting to? What was I meant to be doing again? On my first day, I put on make-up and jeans, even though if anyone saw my bottom half it would mean something had gone really wrong. I read the instructions on how to download all the apps I needed to communicate with the rest of the team. I sat at my computer a full forty-five minutes before my start time. (I guessed my start time was 8.30am, a guess based on nothing.) Within ten minutes of the first morning, I immediately identified the limitations of an online workplace versus a physical workplace: I had no way of knowing who my boss was.

Now, to clarify, I knew who my top, *top* boss was. He was the one who had asked if I was interested in this job in the first place, so I understood that. But aside from him, I didn't have a clue about the hierarchy of this place. When you work in an office, usually the boss has a nicer office than everyone else and wears better-quality jumpers, and in any case, on your first day they often walk up to you and say, 'Hello, I'm the boss,' and then they shake your hand. You may never talk to them again, but you know who they are because of that handshake. I couldn't work out who was senior. I looked at email signatures and found lots of job titles I had never heard of before. I looked at the banter on Slack and tried to identify which banter had a whiff of seniority about it. I thought of sending someone a message saying, *Who is my boss, thanks*, but then didn't know if that would be construed as disrespectful. These people didn't know me. They may have thought I was some sort of anarchist. I decided to treat everyone like they were in charge of me.

Because nobody ever wrote, *I'm taking a lunch break!* on Slack, I didn't eat lunch for the first six days of my new job. This was too embarrassing to confess to any of my colleagues. I would sometimes run from my computer and shove handfuls of popcorn into my mouth and then run back as if they would dock my pay for those thirty seconds. I didn't know when the workday ended at this place, so would just linger on my laptop until I saw the little bulbs next to people's Slack handles dim. In Zoom calls of twenty people, I tried to figure out what everyone did. Everyone else seemed to know each other from the before time, so for them working over video was sort of funny and annoying, not a constant vortex of terror. Everyone seemed so certain of their roles that it was unnecessary to say what they were. I put myself on mute because it seemed safest. There was one woman who stayed silent in all calls, always watching thoughtfully, never laughing. I began to wonder if anyone else could see her.

The first time I was asked to speak in one of these calls (taking myself off mute for the first time in the group chat) was to read out something I had written so that everyone could tell me if it was good or not. Reading out loud on a video call is wonderful if you like the feeling of constantly interrupting people. Suffice to say, it was a disaster: my internet kept freezing and cutting out, I couldn't hear what people were saying and I kept repeating myself. The big boss had to chime in and read parts for me when I became stuck in the digital purgatory of the living and the dead. I felt as though my lack of high-speed internet access was being read as a personal failing. 'Her internet is bad – what else about her is bad, pray tell?' I read faster to get it over with, which I knew meant that no one could really understand what I was saying. As I was finishing the reading, knowing that it wasn't exactly right and may have been impossible to give feedback on, I paused to signal that I was finished. At that same moment, my boyfriend flushed the old toilet in our small apartment, a noise that shook the walls, echoed throughout the rooms and, without a doubt in my mind, would have been audible over this call. *Seems about right,* I thought.

With every Zoom call I became increasingly petrified that I would be called on again. *You look terrified,* someone Slacked me during one of the calls, and I tried to smile to show I wasn't terrified and was actually having a really good time (he could have been my boss, after all). The big, big boss called in my first week, saying that he was sorry I had to learn all these new skills remotely.

'I definitely didn't think I would be asking you to take on a new job during a pandemic,' he said, with a laugh. 'Are you finding the work to be okay?'

'Nah, it's cool!' I said in a voice that was higher than my own. Sensing that calling a pandemic 'cool' isn't really a cool thing to do, I added, 'It's fun!'

'I'm glad that you're, ah, having fun,' the big, big boss said politely.

'HAHAHAHAHA!' I said in reply. We got off the phone. I contemplated sticking my head in a blender.

My contract was only for three months and the three months were a blur of Zoom calls and me asking a lot of questions, probably to the wrong people. *What does that mean?* someone once asked me on Slack, when I asked him a question that made no sense.

I don't know, I wrote back, because I really didn't.

On my last week, I bought myself sunny yellow flowers to congratulate myself for doing something tricky. I may not have gotten the hang of it, but I was bloody glad (and grateful) I'd done it. I knew my younger self – who had dreamed of working at a job like this – would have been proud of me. I wonder if one day I will be walking down the street and recognise someone I saw on one of those Zoom calls. I wonder if they will recognise me. I wonder if they will be my boss. I wonder if when they see me, they will hear a toilet flushing.

The expiration date

Oh, so you've been nominated for a 30 under 30 award?

Congratulations. This is so exciting. This is just the beginning – and yet somehow also the midpoint – for you!

How is it that you are so young and yet so wise? How is it that your exquisite brain and wholesome bones (bones that have *known* things) can be wrapped in such supple, poreless flesh? How is it that your skin, skin without lines except for when you give a knowing smile, can be lightly freckled and yet not damaged? It's really good skin, is what I'm saying.

Your ideas are so future that they can never be *fully* understood and yet are coherent enough for the oldest member of the Media Entertainment & Arts Alliance to relate to. You are exciting but never threatening – like a bazooka dressed in a Minions costume.

Your sentences make people feel as though they are being thrust into outer space.

Your work is infused with the energy of a sixteen-year-old punk, the measured consideration of a fifty-year-old Harvard professor, the old-fashioned whimsy of a young Oscar Wilde, the cutting cultural critique of a writer on the second season of *Seinfeld* and the awe of a baby born half an hour ago.

People often say that you have the same calm reassurance as a thousand-year-old ancient deity, or Sir Ian McKellen.

Your fans are young, groups of kids who you have inspired to turn, as one, away from their screens and towards the intellectual sun, to be warmed and nourished, little tingles of energy rippling along their nerve-endings and a disembodied voice whispering softly in their AirPods, 'There is a tomorrow.'

But your fans are older readers, too, real literary types. They recognise a spark in you, admire your candour, but never believe that your brilliance is menacing in any way. You remind them of a long-lost love that they met at a seaside carnival before the war broke out.

How is any of this possible? How did you get this way? 'Just by listening,' you say with a shy smile, to an eager crowd watching you at the Opera House. 'Listening and actually hearing.' Everyone erupts into rabid applause, a feverish mania the likes of which haven't been seen since Harry Styles grazed his crotch with his hand on stage in 2013. Everyone quote-tweets you, in a nice way. You're being interviewed by Leigh Sales.

When people ask to adapt your work – which is often – you say slowly, 'I don't know ... I don't have a TV?' and then look curiously at your agent and your manager, both of whom are over thirty and own multiple TVs.

Awards aren't important to you, but if they were important, it would be because being acknowledged as advanced while you are in your twenties (the 'game-changer' stage of your career, as we call it in the biz) is absolutely paramount and an indicator of your future success. You think you can create great art *after* that? In your thirties, with your wisps of baby grey hairs and your hangovers and all those wedding invitations? Haha.

Yes, sure, Jack Kerouac published *On the Road* at thirty-five, but did he go to an award ceremony? Get his photo put in a nice magazine? Huh? Huh? He didn't.

NO IT DOES NOT MATTER THAT NORA EPHRON WAS IN HER FORTIES WHEN SHE PUBLISHED *HEARTBURN*; YOU ARE COMPLETELY MISSING THE POINT OF THIS EXERCISE.

If you have not published an intimidatingly superb piece of work before the morning of your thirtieth birthday, you are kaput! This is the deadline! Without the deadline we wouldn't know what to strive for! We'd all be flopping around like beached jellyfish! We'd all be wallowing in champagne rivers like slovenly French dukes! We need this deadline! We need to measure the work in this way!

What's the point otherwise!!!

What's the point!!!

On cooking

Of all the movies that I pretend I've never seen voluntarily, *Eat Pray Love* has to be the worst one. I hate *Eat Pray Love*. I *despise* it. Watching it is akin to shaving your eyeballs with tiny razors. It's the same sensation as biting your tongue and then immediately stubbing your toe, and someone seeing all that play out then yelling, 'ARE YOU OKAY?' It's a heap of Pears-soap-scented, privileged nonsense that is drenched in superiority and white-saviour complexes – a movie so bad that even Julia Roberts and Viola Davis can't save it. It's bad.

Okay. Is everyone gone now? I watch *Eat Pray Love* at least once a year, and I know the exact reason why. It's not because I love seeing Julia Roberts crying on the floor and asking God to tell her if she should get a divorce, or when she steals her boyfriend's spiritual guru (she has enough money to visit the guru's ashram in India; her boyfriend does not) or when she contemplates buying a new pair of jeans because she has put on weight after finally developing an appetite for food and life. Maybe other women like these bits, and that's their own business. I like plenty of things that are bad for me. I am in no position to judge.

But the reason *I* have seen *Eat Pray Love* so many times, is a specific scene when Julia Roberts is in Italy. In the previous scene, some Italians have been mocking her because she is American and thus is such a capitalist automaton that she doesn't understand the 'sweetness of doing nothing'. To prove to herself that she *does* understand the sweetness of doing nothing, one afternoon, Julia Roberts puts on a negligee even though there is no sexual partner around to see her wearing a negligee and cooks herself the following meal: a hard-boiled egg that has been salt-and-peppered and sliced in two, a chunk of crusty bread, a few spears of asparagus (covered in olive oil), a lump of soft cheese, two olives, some grapes and a sliver of prosciutto. She eats with her hands while sitting on the floor (there is a chair right next to her, but sitting on a chair is not a very earthy thing to do).

Since I first saw this movie almost ten years ago, I have thought about this meal approximately once a week. It seems to me the most decadent and luxurious meal that I have ever seen. This is because it is a meal without any regard for leftovers. It's *expensive* *. It has a decidedly 'serves one' vibe, but not in a Lean Cuisine frozen-meal way. This is a meal you make alone in an apartment in Rome, with the shutters open and the sun

---

*   Asparagus is expensive; I'm not an heiress.

pouring in. The bubble of the pot when the egg is being boiled! The crack of its shell! The glug of the olive oil drenching the asparagus! How that slice of salmon (or prosciutto, which I prefer) shines! The way everything is arranged in a rustic heap, a perfect symphony of textures and temperatures.

The best bit about this meal is that it takes absolutely no skill to cook it.

While I have been able to recreate this meal without difficulty – I realise it would be a real worry if I could not boil an egg – I have never felt the pull to cook anything particularly complex. I have a few go-to meals up my sleeve: a carbonara; pancakes; a smoked paprika-y chickpea-and-sweet-potato situation; roast pork with crackling; a dahl that I have made exactly twice. This isn't one of those insufferable 'How do you adult!?' things, because I *can* cook if I have to. I just find the whole thing boring. It's not relaxing. I just don't *care*.

I don't care about making risotto. I don't dream about sourdough starters. I wrongly assumed that the run of everyone getting breadmakers in the '90s, and then promptly realising that the process was laborious and you needed too many ingredients and the bread was somehow too crunchy and too glue-y at the same time, had purged us of those desires. (One of my old housemates had a breadmaker, and after a disastrous attempt at baking a mixed-grain loaf, managed to burn rock-hard bread dough into the machine and couldn't seem to clean it out, no matter how hard she chipped away at it. She left it sitting on the kitchen bench for several weeks. The burned bread began to smell, and she eventually threw the whole machine away.)

A few months into 2020, all of my social-media feeds were full of two things: brands assuring me that they would look after their customers during this 'unprecedented time' (by providing free shipping for their $80 candles) and people posting pictures of sourdough bread. We had to channel our sadness and anxiety into bread. I felt very sad and very anxious, but I really didn't want to make sourdough. The only time I had tried to make bread was in Grade Three, when one of the mums, the wife of a famous Melbourne chef who had a glittery restaurant on Bourke Street, had come to give us a baking demonstration in the hall. 'Did you know that yeast is alive?' she told my class. I was aghast. While my classmates spent the rest of the hour kneading dough and splattering white flour on each other, I stood still at my table, watching a lump of yeast from the corner of my eye and waiting for it to try to crawl slowly off the table.

Perhaps the reason I have never been especially drawn to cooking is that I grew up around excellent cooks. Good food was pretty much always in my grasp without me having to lift a finger. I knew I should have been ashamed by this fact, and I was. My mum is a great cook, and so was her mother. Grandma's large, spotless kitchen always seemed to have a pot boiling or meat roasting or a kettle that was whistling. It was all very delightful. As soon as my cousins and I would arrive at her house we would be given 'jobs': deliberately easy tasks that would not allow us to stuff up the cooking process (putting napkins in napkin rings or placing a glob of butter on top of a pile of steaming peas etc.).

My grandma would make tureens of buttery baby potatoes covered in parsley; moist chicken and sweet ham; loaves of malty soda bread; stuffing full of juicy cranberries (that's right, my family is white!); and trifles that elevated sponge cake, jelly and jam to the realms of Michelin stars. She would whip all of these up while wearing a delicate string of pearls and a soft cashmere twin-set that she would never spill anything on. The food that my grandma made wasn't fancy, but it still felt sophisticated somehow. One of the dishes that my cousins and I loved the most was grandma's pasta salad, a fresh mix of buttery penne, green olives, sundried tomato, capsicum and parsley. She made it every Christmas, and there were never any leftovers. She knew what to cook for every situation and never seemed to incorrectly guess the mood of the meal.

Since my mum did all of the cooking when I was growing up, I only learned how when I moved out of home. My mum is a very resilient woman and completely devoted to caring for every single person around her, resulting in myself and my siblings happily lacking any real life skills for the first twenty years of our existence. I have a vivid memory of my sister and me being hungry specifically for a chocolate slice, so we decided to make a packet-mix hedgehog that had been gathering dust in the cupboard.

'You two are cooking, are you?' said my mother, scoffing, which naturally enraged us.

We, of course, got distracted – I think maybe the Teen Choice Awards were on – and accidentally forgot to add butter to the slice. Rather than lose face in front of our mum, we whispered, 'Deny the truth,' to each other like a pact, threw the slice out and pretended we'd eaten it all.

Andy does most of the cooking in our house. For him it actually *is* relaxing – he listens to podcasts while he lovingly grates and slices and sautés. Nothing seems to dampen his love of cooking. Once he sliced off the tip of his thumb while making us souvlakis, but we managed to stem the bleeding pretty quickly. He briefly considered training to be a chef in high school, before realising that working in a commercial kitchen was very hot and involved people yelling at you a lot, two situations he finds almost unbearable. My mum, who still seems to struggle to accept that I have a handle on basic life skills, talks to him about recipes and gives him tips, assuming that he is the one who keeps us alive on a day-to-day basis. It's only really annoying when she also solely talks to him about washing products and stain-removal techniques, as if I am so incompetent that I can't be relied on to cook *or* clean in our household, like I am just a helpless baby lying in a bathrobe all day, waiting to be spoon-fed peeled grapes. That doesn't sound like a bad existence, but it's just not the whole story.

Whenever I cook for Andy, I get frustrated that it never tastes as good as the things that he whips up.

'Why doesn't this taste like the food you make?' I asked one day, while we were chewing on a lacklustre broccolini pasta I had just overcooked. 'What do you add that makes it taste so much better than my bland food?'

He paused for a minute, frowning. 'Salt?' he said innocently. I didn't make the broccolini pasta for a while.

I do wish I found joy in the cooking process, because it sounds great. To have a terrible day and then come home and make a four-layer sponge cake with jam and cream and pink icing, and then with each delicious bite forget all your troubles (court cases, tax debts, estranged relatives, witches' curses etc.) and feeling proud that you took a bunch of different-coloured sands and waters and managed to make something sweet.

'I'm going to bake soda bread!' I announced one morning in May, having been locked inside for going on three months.

'Great!' Andy said, seemingly relieved that I was still motivated enough to do positive tasks, instead of spending my days sporadically bursting into tears, feverishly FaceTiming my family and pacing the apartment in a drunken daze.

'Great!' I said back. I marched to the supermarket to buy wholemeal flour and sugar and 'baking soda', and when the supermarket had none of these things, I marched back home, sat on the couch and watched four hours of an American drama about teenage drug addicts. I lit some incense so it felt more purposeful.

A week later, I decided that maybe my best option was a sweet starter cake like banana bread.

It's more of a science experiment, I texted in a group chat, when I needed to ask my baking friends a question about grams and cups. Baking is a subculture that I understood to be optimistic, but also judgemental. If I phrased it as an experiment, then it was funny – and not devastating – if I managed to bake a banana-scented brick.

'I don't care if it tastes good, okay???' I said to Andy roughly, while advising him that yes, I would be using up the bunch of bananas he had bought for his breakfasts.

'Okay,' he said, and left the room quietly.

I'm going to bake banana bread, are you shocked? I texted my family group chat.

Yuck, my sister texted back. *I would never eat banana or a banana product.* She hated bananas. I suddenly remembered that I too hated bananas. Why was I doing this?

It's more of a science experiment, I texted back.

What did this domestic urge mean? Was I again looking to my peers for guidance as to how I needed to improve? Had I not previously prided myself on eschewing anything domestic and, let's face it, useful? Was it possible that everything I thought I knew about myself was false? That now I was stuck inside, my confinement was revealing a truth that was more horrifying and confusing than I could ever imagine? That I had secretly always wanted to be a *casual baker*?

I am an enthusiastic eater – albeit an unadventurous one – and have had intense love affairs with particular dishes. (A list of specific dishes I have had love affairs with: a plate of burrata and sweet tomato; apple crumble with cream, eaten at breakfast; a medium-rare steak with cauliflower cheese; a katsu curry; a well-timed Kingston biscuit; potato pierogi; a Moroccan chickpea bake; a fried chicken sandwich in Auckland that cured a hangover; a bowl of Persian jewelled rice and roasted kumara.) But cooking is not therapy to me. I go to therapy for therapy. I can see how that is not as wholesome.

The last few Christmases have been strange for my family. Both my grandparents passed away, and so did my aunt. The rest of the family meets like we always have, eating ham and turkey and buttery potatoes. My mum does a lot of the cooking now, usually in her sweltering kitchen on a 35-plus degree day, which is very stressful. Because of this, for the last few years I have been in charge of making grandma's pasta salad – it's not like I could be trusted with the turkey. But I had two hands and a workable brain, so I was an acceptable candidate. I sliced green olives, shredded parsley, scattered the oil in the sundried tomato jar over the pasta, sometimes fielding concerned looks from my mum, who was trying to shove a turkey half her size into the oven.

'Yay, Grandma's pasta salad!' said my cousin Cora, when it was time to eat later that night.

'Sinéad made it,' my sister said.

'… What?' said my cousin Harry in concern, as if we had just announced that we'd be taking the ham, rolling it on the street for a while, sticking some used syringes in and then presenting it on the table. I made a big deal of pretending I was offended that they all thought I could fuck up a dish that only involved boiling pasta, but was also a little bit worried that I *had* fucked it and effectively ruined our childhood.

My cousins and I piled our plates and sat down at the smaller table next to my aunty Anne's dining room table – a table that had always been 'the kids table', but this day was hosting a bunch of thirty-somethings and their thirty-something partners.

'This is great!' Harry said.

'Very good,' said my cousin Kate.

Everyone was piling the penne into their gobs. I had a taste of it myself. It did taste pretty good.

'It's very simple,' I said, just in case everyone thought I now considered myself some culinary genius.

'Nah, but that's why it's good,' my other cousin James said, with his mouth full.

The banana bread turned out okay, too. Actually it was better than okay – it was delicious, and we ate the whole thing in two days. Because I am but a predictable woman of flesh, blood, bone, with access to an Alison Roman cookbook and the *Smitten Kitchen* website, as three months inside stretched to eight months on and off of lockdown (mostly on – I didn't trust our brief easing of restrictions a couple of months in and only ate two restaurant meals out – a huge blunder in retrospect) I did bake a few more things for the first time: scones, blondies and a lemon turmeric teacake, all famous for how easy they are to make. I knew I was doing it because I needed to feel productive and not because I enjoyed it. They all tasted delicious. Baking is boring.

Fatal defects
(or the life skills I have no
reason not to have)

The bike thing

There is a passage in the New Testament in which Jesus Christ sits down in an olive grove and says to his gathered apostles, 'Guys, I decided a new rule this morning.'

'Okay, lay it on us,' the gathered apostles ask, ready to commit the new rule to memory so later on when they're at the market they can tell people off for not following the new rule.

'Okay, here it is,' says Jesus leaning forward, his hands gripping his thighs in excitement. 'If you don't know how to ride a bike, you are an idiot swine who belongs in hell.'

This is a lie, because bikes weren't invented until 1817 – also I don't know if Jesus actually used phrases like 'idiot swine who belongs in hell' because I don't know if he was that good at branding – but the sentiment is surely true. Somewhere in history, it was decided that if you had the physical ability to ride a bike, then you had to know how to ride a bike. I don't know when this happened, but it certainly happened. At some point – and again and again throughout time – there was some sort of unspoken contract that everyone would know how to ride a bike. They would just *know*. And no one ever talks about it.

Hey, it must be wonderful. To just hop on your bike and pedal and pedal while the wind whips your hair and the sun warms your back and the ground falls below your feet, and suddenly you're in the sky, suddenly you're pedalling so hard that you are in space, suddenly you are surrounded by stars, suddenly the oxygen has disappeared, suddenly you're choking and – basically, I don't know what it feels like to ride a bike.

It wasn't until I was a teenager that I realised that not knowing how to ride a bike was a baffling hole in my life skills. I used to think it was quite normal, like not being able to rollerblade or make your own dinner. Then it suddenly became clear that every single person I knew, knew how to ride a bike and had known how to do it practically since birth. *When did that happen?* Was there some compulsory bike training program I missed out on as a child?

The first time I decided that I needed to fix the bike issue was before Year Nine camp, when I realised that despite picking the least physically demanding camp on offer, I still had to participate in a one-hour nature bike ride. My dad offered to teach me with a rusty hand-me-down bike we had in the garage and, let me tell you, there is nothing that exacerbates tensions between a fourteen-year-old girl and her father more than that experience. I think I tried for fifteen minutes and then threw the bike down on a football field and stomped back home. While the rest of my camp was on the nature bike ride, I joined up with the neighbouring horse-riding camp for a high-ropes course, which I also hated.

The maths thing

In my head, I can invent complex scenarios that never actually took place. I can vividly imagine the setting, what was said, how everyone was dressed, the looks on their faces. I am so good at fabricating past events – almost always involving me being found out for making a grave error, like talking too much rubbish at a party, saying something hurtful by accident or dropping a priceless Ming vase – that sometimes I can convince myself that they really happened. I can create entire alternative histories and complex timelines; I can rewrite every social situation I have ever experienced in my life and construct complete universes – but I can't do maths in my head.

I have never really been interested in maths, so never tried that hard at it at school. In Year Ten, some sort of clerical error resulted in me being put into the advanced maths class, but after two lessons of me staring slack-jawed at the whiteboard and wondering why the teacher was talking in ancient Greek, I realised that I wasn't suitable for the rigours of the curriculum.

From then on I never trusted my capacity to manage numbers. At my hospitality job, I opted to work in the kitchens rather than at the till, less disgusted by the idea of pulling the guts out of raw chickens than by the possibility of having to work out change on the spot. When the bill comes at the end of a meal, I use the calculator on my phone to work out the split, making sure to do it discretely under the table. I get nervous during pay negotiations, not because I worry about seeming greedy or pig-headed, but because I know I am so confounded by numbers that I could accidentally agree to something that doesn't serve me, just because I don't know what 'per annum' means.

Sometimes, when I am feeling bold and like I could enter, improved, into a new stage of life, I try to practise doing mental maths instead of automatically reaching for my phone. One Christmas, my boyfriend and I were given *The Barefoot Investor*; it was during that summer when everyone seemed to be splitting their money into four accounts and smugly flashing an orange bank card like they had discovered the secret to wealth. I opened the book once, read half a page, then read *The Girl on the Train* instead.

I still haven't read *The Barefoot Investor*. We use it to prop up a photo of us at The Wizarding World of Harry Potter at Universal Studios in Florida. I have no idea how we afforded that holiday.

The car thing

Not being able to drive a car is the sort of thing you could probably pass off as a political statement, but unfortunately I have never been able to pull this off. *I'm doing it for the* climate, I have thought about saying, but I know my hypocrisy in the general 'saving the planet' area would quickly be found out.

I don't know why I didn't learn to drive a car. When I was a teenager, I just took the bus to places. Now I just take the tram to places. Am I an unambitious hound? There's a very good chance.

I know not having a licence is a fatal personality defect, because my eyes work fine and I still haven't done it. It might be laziness, or my fear that I'll be driving on a bridge one day and my brain will just go berserk and I'll drive off the side. 'Haha,' my brain will say, as if it was a prank. But it won't be a good prank: I will be dead! It's important to treat your brain as if it is separate from you; like it's a malevolent devil who constantly dares you to do risky and destructive things while the rest of your body clutches its pearls in shock. So to speak.

I don't really ask for lifts to places, but whenever I am given a lift I do feel an acute sense of shame. My friend Sez, who often drives me places (places that she is also going to – I'm not like, 'Hey Sez, can you take me to this party? You're not invited, btw'), doesn't even let me navigate, as if my inability to drive a car means I am also unable to read a map. She's right about this, of course, but there's an injustice to it all the same.

If you cannot drive a car (and don't have a super good reason for this) and have been in a position where you have to disclose this in a social situation, you will know that the reaction from other people is always the same. 'How?!' people around you will say, and then they look at each other and say, 'How?!' and everyone starts smiling in a confused way, and many shoulders are shrugging, and they all start looking at you as if you've been in a bomb shelter for sixty years and have emerged wearing bell-bottoms and a peace-sign necklace and are asking them how the overthrow of Castro went. When two people who can't drive cars find each other – which is very rare, because admitting that you can't drive a car is embarrassing – they can almost trick themselves into thinking that they've fallen in love.

Every Christmas, my aunty Anne asks, 'Do you know how to drive yet?' and laughs before I answer. I wonder, if I won a Nobel Peace Prize, whether she would ask if I know how to drive a car yet, or just question how I actually got to the award ceremony. Last Christmas, the mockery got worse because someone even more powerful than Aunty Anne joined the fray: my mum. 'Your little sister might drive a car before you do!' she said with a laugh.

But guess what? My little sister is in her mid-twenties and still doesn't know how to drive a car either.

Help!

I will read every single 'How to Be Better at XXX' article you send me. I will bookmark it. I will take *handwritten notes*. I will study it like a Catholic child in Grade Four looking for the vulgar bits of the Bible in between the complicated bits about how we're sinners even when we're babies. I will make it my religion.

I will read about the morning rituals of CEOs, productivity tips from artists and skincare regimes/breakfast sandwich recipes from celebrity psychologists. I will try to incorporate these tips into my commute, into my lunch break, into my friendship catch-ups, into phone calls with my family and during my sleep. Maybe if you saw me slumbering, I would be knitting in my sleep (mindfulness!) or doing yoga poses (fitness!) or writing a short story for no one else, just for me (creativity should be a gift to yourself!). I don't have a camera in my room, so I can't tell you for sure. My boyfriend might be able to tell you, but he is a heavy sleeper and, in any case, he probably hasn't read all of the articles that I have read so wouldn't understand the deep importance of my deeply healthy rituals.

I don't know a lot about self-help books, not because I am healthy but because I don't have the attention span to read them. I have *tried*; boy, have I tried. I once bought *The Happiness Trap* because being happy sounded like an absolutely delightful, if quaint, thing to be. (I ignored the 'trap' part.) I bought *Quiet* by Susan Cain to make myself feel better about being an introvert and less inclined to 'betray' myself by giving away my 'recharge time', despite still feeling like if I cancelled a plan out of tiredness the world would explode and the skin would fry and sizzle off our bones and we'd all be dead dead dead but I would still be conscious enough to know that it was all my fault.

I don't think I read more than a chapter of either.

I do have some positive associations with the whole self-help book industry, though. Back when I worked late nights at Borders, I would sometimes hide in the self-help section when I was tired of approaching customers and begging them to buy something. I would squat between two tall shelves stuffed with dusty books called *Get Organised – Now!* or *Stop Feeling Sad!* and pretend to be looking for something whenever my manager walked past. It was a very big store, so I could usually keep that going for about forty-five minutes, particularly if it was after 9pm, an unwholesome time to be buying self-help books. Customers barely ever entered the section, and when they did, they went straight for the book they wanted and scurried out – as if I was going to stop them, inspect the book they had picked up and then loudly exclaim, 'RIGHT – YOU'VE GOT TROUBLE GETTING SOMEONE TO LOVE YA, DO YA?'

The self-help section was next to the cooking section – which seemed to me like very passive-aggressive genre placement, because cooking well is hard and we all know it – so while I was squatting in the self-help aisle I could also watch videos of Jamie Oliver making Christmas hams or Nigella Lawson cooking biscuits made out of chocolate bars. Sometimes, the old Italian men, who hung out together in the store late at night and read magazines they never bought, gave me Ferrero Rochers to eat while I sat on my invisible chair and watched the cooking shows. I was never tempted to crack the spine on any of the mountains of self-help books that surrounded me, though given my lax work ethic, perhaps it would have been a good idea.

The self-help advice of Instagram psychologists, however, has had much more of an impact on me. I love to see their tiles appear in my newsfeed: tiles with graphics ranging from minimalist custom type on chic blocks of emerald or navy, to swirly self-care statements on cream rectangles with a blurry background photo of a woman walking on an empty beach. Instagram psychologists only dole out advice via either a graphic designer's business card or the cover of a romance novel from the 1980s. There is no in between.

Instagram psychologists have explained boundaries to me and given me phrases to try out whenever I am confronted with someone who is taking an emotional jackhammer to my boundaries (like, 'No, thank you!'), and they've told me how bad it is that I like the feeling of fixing other people's problems. They have handles like 'Spirituality Susan' and 'Holding Space Hannah'. They say soothing and grandiose things about my ego and how 'the ego knows', and even though I don't really know what 'the ego' is, I suddenly imagine it as a buxom woman with bleach-blonde pin-curls in a floor-length gold gown, swaddled by a mink coat that seems to be perpetually falling off her shoulders. My ego says things like, 'Darling – it's five o'clock somewhere!' as she sips a martini at 11am and never sits on chairs, only pianos, and has been married five times and widowed in 'mysterious circumstances' four of those times.

The only problem is that the more Instagram psychologists I follow, the more I am confronted with different philosophies of living, the more I start to feel like I'm behind on emotional homework. I've taken notes, I've saved posts, I've screenshotted so many tiles that my phone has become too clogged to download any more podcasts, and who knows how to use the iCloud anyway? It's gotten dire.

I know I don't need these slogans, and that they're just gentle reminders rather than commandments to live by if you wish to succeed (the Ten Commandments, another complicated bit of the Bible). But there is comfort in someone telling you what to do, because survival can feel quite, quite difficult sometimes. I mean, I'm fine! It's just that sometimes it does feel like the expectations of the people I know and the people I know on the internet and the people I haven't even met yet but who still expect something are crushing me like bricks made out of mercury, but I can't *really* focus on that because I'm so busy 'Leaning In' that I am perpetually at a right angle, just leaning and leaning and leaning, until my face and my knees touch and my butt becomes my face and I lean into the core of the earth and become a fungus statue like in *Annihilation*. But I'm okay – *look at all of these self-help slogans I've screenshotted; look, it's the background of my phone!*

I can understand why so many of my friends have turned to astrology apps to make sense of it all, believing that our glittering, ancient cosmos can offer more insights into the human condition than any individual person could. I've done the same myself. The only problem is that for every warm rush of identification sparked by an accurate star-sign meme, you must also reckon with the raw chaos of a robotic app sending you patronising and sometimes menacing push notifications.

Everything doesn't happen for a reason, everything happens because it happens, period, an astrology app once told me. *Don't be sneaky*, it said another day, as if it had seen all the texts and notes and messages in my phone, which was the same as seeing into my soul, and had found it all to be quite sneaky. *God didn't create humans, humans created God*, was another puzzling one.

What does this mean? my sister once texted me, along with a screenshot of her astrology app advising her, one Thursday at 10.42am to *hold two opposing ideas in your brain all day*. It was hard enough to hold *one* idea in your brain – now we were all expected to have two at any given time? I imagined that all of this advice was being written by a giant old man Zeus made out of stars, who was sitting in a chair made of suns and trying to get us all to do the stupidest things for his entertainment, because space can be quite boring sometimes.

The aim of following all these Instagram accounts and downloading these apps is to make me a better and more mentally balanced person, but given how much of it hinges on how to deal with other people's bad behaviour, I do have some fears about becoming *too* mentally balanced. What if I follow more and more and more psychologists until my whole feed is just filled up with advice about how I am always right and the others are always wrong and it makes me *too* confident and *too* secure and pretty soon I am an arsehole? What if every time someone does something I don't like (cracks their knuckles, recites an entire scene from *The Simpsons* etc.) I get to tell them off because of boundaries, or something? What if I become the sort of person who says things like, 'It's self-care time, bitches!'? What if I decide that self-care is about nourishing yourself, no matter the cost? Skip that line! Keep that wallet you found on the tram! Steal other people's lunches! Ignore your loved ones when they ask for a kidney, and refuse to feel bad for being the kind of person who just *likes* the feeling of having two kidneys! Giving away a kidney is the enemy of self-care!

Is it possible to get *too* healthy? I am scared to find out.

Strangely, the ideas I have found most comforting don't come from books or slogans by experts who have figured it all out but from people who have made a real mess of things and just sort of raised their arms in a shrug and got on with it. The book *Adult Fantasy* by Briohny Doyle – which is about how the traditional markers for adulthood have changed, which is why many adults feel like they are just pretending – made me feel much better about not knowing how to do things that other thirty-year-olds seemed to know how to do. In her song called 'Pilot', the musician Aldous Harding sings in a strange strangled voice: 'I get so anxious I need a tattoo / Something binding, that hides me,' which was the sort of embarrassing feeling I felt when I got my second tattoo, though I couldn't quite define it then. The poet Frank O'Hara wrote things about feeling nervous and restless and like everything that was happening around him was sort of boring, and he did it in a way that is so funny and beautiful that reading his work feels like my brain is being zapped with electric currents. He was part of the 'New York School' of poets in the 1950s and '60s, until he was hit by a car in 1966 and died. He had worked at the Museum of Modern Art in New York, first at the information desk in the lobby and later as a curator of painting and sculpture (he had no formal training), and would write poems on his lunch break. His 1964 book *Lunch Poems* was the first collection of poetry I ever owned. His poetry has nothing to do with self-help, but somehow it's helped me make sense of things.

The first thing of Frank O'Hara's I ever read (which I discovered on Instagram, in between boundaries tiles) was a bit from his poem 'Mayakovsky':

Now I am quietly waiting for
the catastrophe of my personality
to seem beautiful again,
and interesting, and modern.

There has barely been a day since where 'catastrophe of my personality' doesn't roll around my head, or sit on my tongue like a toffee melting in my mouth. It makes me think that Frank would probably find self-help books boring, too.

Three doctors

The second I enter a doctor's consulting room, I suddenly feel free of all symptoms. It doesn't matter how sick I felt that morning, or on the commute, or in the waiting room. I could be vomiting blood or have a throbbing cut on my finger that is full of pus. I could have a case of thrush so bad that I have fantasies of what my life would be like if I carved my body in half just below the bellybutton. I am probably a medical marvel, but I don't know for sure.

Whenever I began an appointment with my GP, Dr Wing, a great sense of wellness would suddenly descend upon my body, as if all my organs were pausing and holding their breath until I left the room, at which point they could exhale and start aching again.

It's not even like Dr Wing had an extraordinarily comforting bedside manner. He was not an unkind doctor, but he did sometimes make a disgusted face like he was a more popular

246

Year Ten girl being forced to be your partner in PE. I just always suspected I was wasting his time.

One time it felt as though all the pipes in my torso were clogged with spiders, so I went to Dr Wing to see if he could do something about it. 'My ears really are very blocked!' I said in a weak voice, justifying this nonsense visit. 'And my chest, it feels blocked too and maybe … my head?' I placed my hand lightly on my chest, as if trying to prove how fragile and vulnerable I was. Now that I had convinced myself I wasn't really sick and was making a fuss out of nothing (my organs were still holding their breath) I thought that the least I could do was give Dr Wing a bit of a show. 'I'm sure it'll go away soon,' I said. 'But it has felt like this for a while!' I added, in case he might push a panic button under his desk to summon the pseudoephedrine police.

Dr Wing was the sort of man who could either be twenty-five or forty. He was very neat and tidy and had an orderly desk. I didn't know anything about him, which I guess is normal, but strange when you think about how much he knew about me. I'm used to being the one asking questions in social situations. He was very softly spoken but would sometimes look at me with a scrunched face like I was concerningly dim, like the time I asked him if it was bad that I hadn't gotten any vaccinations for a trip to Bali the day before I took a trip to Bali.

'Ah yes,' said Dr Wing kindly on the spider-torso day, 'a lot of people have been coming in with symptoms like that.' He searched my ears for spiders and then typed out a prescription for a spider-killing antihistamine. 'Lots of blocked ears lately – and diarrhoea.'

'Oh, really?' I said in a voice I hope faked polite curiosity. 'That sounds bad.' He agreed that it was pretty bad. I felt myself shift uncomfortably in my seat, like I was absorbing all the diarrhoea germs from butts of the past. Ear and chest congestion suddenly didn't seem so bad.

'I had food poisoning last week,' said Dr Wing, still wanting to discuss diarrhoea.

'Oh yeah?' I said. This was the most he had ever confided in me. My organs continued to hold their breath.

'Yes. I was at a volleyball tournament and all I ate all day was a piece of salmon sushi. I got home at 5.30 and spent the next twenty-four hours thinking I was dying.' He shook his head wearily, like a man forced to relive the consequences of the single worst decision of his life. He adjusted his glasses and handed me the prescription. I asked if we could also make a mental health plan while we were there. It had been a hard few weeks for us all.

The day I realised that my psychologist was the smartest and meanest person on planet earth was the day I admitted one of the darkest, mollusc-glued-to-my-heart kind of beliefs, and she laughed and said, 'Okay, do you really think you are *that* smart and everyone you've ever met is *that* dumb and you've somehow managed to fool them all?' It was a real moment.

Jill didn't suffer fools, which was exciting, as I had often acted like a fool and wondered if I would get away with it forever. She was energetic, honest and frequently peppered her advice with anecdotes about times she had acted badly and gotten over it, usually explaining the situation while waving her hands in the air. 'You know, I might do it again – and that's fine!' she'd say in a loud voice with her arms waving like she was pulling an invisible slinky between her hands.

Even though I had been seeing her for years, I was so concerned about impressing her that I spent about thirty minutes before every appointment writing down exactly what I wanted to talk about, lest there be a lull in our conversation that might lead her to think I was wasting her time. (I was also aware that I was only allotted a certain number of subsidised appointments a year – wasting mental health appointments is the domain of millionaire playboys.)

One tumultuous summer, when I kept saying things like, 'I can't go outside!' and, 'Maybe I should never speak to anyone ever again!' I walked into the reception of Jill's office feeling more depleted than ever before. I hadn't even written down talking points because I didn't have the energy. As I dragged myself in, like a snail carrying her home and leaving a slimy trail of misery in her wake, I found an unusual scene. Instead of bounding down the staircase and yelling 'LET'S GO!' when my appointment time had come, Jill was already standing awkwardly in the reception area, staring out the window. She had an uncharacteristically meek expression and her arms hung limply by her sides.

'Something bad has happened,' she said quietly.

Before we go on, it's important to note that Jill was the sort of person who refused to be shocked. That's what it felt like, in any case. She had been a psychologist for years – and not just for little bitches like me. She had worked with prisoners and victims of crime and in law-enforcement forensics departments. She had encountered every human trauma you would fear dreaming about, all the while keeping a cool head and flailing her arms around to demonstrate that we're all capable of bad things. (I imagine she encountered quite a sliding scale of 'bad things' in her career, though. I wonder where my 'thinking uncharitable thoughts about other writers' bad thing ranked.) I could imagine her standing in the wreckage of a city, skyscrapers lying in heaps around her, and frowning at Godzilla while he had pieces of buildings in his hands and people's legs hanging out of his giant mouth, and she'd say, 'Okay. What was that for?' while Godzilla felt ashamed.

As we walked up the stairs to her office, Jill told me in a flat voice what had transpired. She had been drinking peppermint tea in her cosy armchair, opposite the other cosy armchair where her patients usually sat. It had been a quiet morning, as I was her first patient after her month-long Christmas holiday. Her office had two floor-to-ceiling windows, many candles of varying sizes, two boxes of tissues and several clusters of small figurines of friendly animals.

On this day, however, there was something else in the room. Jill had looked up and noticed a small black spider sliding on a single string from the back of the wall-set air conditioner, like it was bungee jumping from a cliff. Jill, who it turned out was petrified of spiders, bolted to her desk drawer where she kept a large can of bug spray. From a comfortable distance, she blasted the spider with a bit more spray than was strictly necessary. The spider halted and started doing that sad spasm thing spiders do when they're sprayed.

But that wasn't all: as Jill sprayed, other tiny spiders began spilling out from behind the air conditioner. It turned out that an entire spider colony had moved into the cosy contours of the unused air conditioner during the Christmas break – a very ambitious time to seek out real estate. As they spewed out, presumably very angry at the murder of their brethren (and who could blame them – even if he was the Fredo, it's a loss) they scuttled out onto the wall and slid down on strings. Suddenly there were so many spiders that the wall appeared speckled with large splodges of black paint – and they were moving fast. Jill started spraying with abandon, drenching the wall in poison and watching as the desperate spiders suffocated enmasse, rendering her office a massive spider battlefield that would surely be discussed solemnly in spider history books for decades to come.

Jill took me into her office to observe the damage. She stood by the door while I went in for a closer look at this twisted mobile of dead spiders hanging off webs. 'Is this some sort of psychological test?' I asked, because I wanted her to like me. 'Are you monitoring my reaction to all these dead baby spiders?'

Jill didn't laugh. 'Let's do the session in the spare room,' she said.

Once we were settled in the new room, Jill seemed distracted. She would occasionally twitch, her eyes sporadically darting up to the corners of the ceiling.

'You're thinking about the spiders, aren't you?' I asked.

Jill sighed. 'I suppose. What were the ethics of killing those spiders?' she said, waving one raised hand and shrugging. 'Could I have attempted to relocate them outside?'

'I don't think you need to feel bad about this one,' I said.

She began the session properly, occasionally looking over her shoulder and absentmindedly brushing imaginary spiders off her arms.

My teeth have always been an issue – more of an emotional issue than anything. I was once told by a dentist that the reason I have a white stripe across my front two teeth is that there was an excess of fluoride in the water of the suburb I lived in while my adult teeth were developing. I don't know if this is true, but it was nice to have something to blame.

'Your teeth are yellow!' a French girl once said to me while pushing me down an embankment in Grade Four, and she was right. It was a pretty good sledge. Bleaching them would do nothing, I was told. I forgot about the stripe while I had my braces on, but when I was cut free in Year Ten, I was scandalised to find they were still there.

'Maybe it makes me more distinctive,' I said to my friends at school, trying not to lose face in the wake of my straight, discoloured teeth. 'Makes me seem like I have … charisma?'

'I think you mean "character",' said my friend Chelsea, while avoiding looking at my teeth. The group was silent. No one wants to have character in Year Ten.

After having the unfortunate experience of needing an emergency root canal while holidaying in Berlin (I didn't realise it was a root canal until I Google Translated the receipt the next day – it certainly explains why it took so long and why the drugs they pumped into me made the three-hour Third Reich walking tour I went on immediately after the operation seem very visceral) I knew I needed to find a proper dentist when I got back to Melbourne. My boyfriend's mum suggested her dentist – he was close to my office, was nice with nervous patients (which I never had been until the Germans hacked into my molars) and wasn't that expensive.

Dr James Con was the chattiest dentist I had ever encountered. It didn't matter if my tongue was numb or if he was scooping out pulp in the middle of my dead tooth, Dr Con would try to engage me in conversation for the entire time I was in the chair. 'What do you reckon about cronuts, Sinéad?' he would ask me as a poker whizzed in my mouth. 'Do you think that *Married at First Sight* is real or fake?' he would wonder aloud, as he pressed a needle into my jaw. He was probably trying to keep me calm, but sometimes he would ask me a particularly thought-provoking question, and I would try to answer and end up saying, 'Nhajj ja,' and just dribbling down my chin. At this stage, the dental nurse would say, 'Cronuts are overrated!' to allow me a reprieve.

I was so grateful to Dr Con for getting me past my terrible root-canal recovery that I decided not only would I visit him again, but I would do so every six months as recommended. As the appointments became less dramatic and more about general teeth maintenance, Dr Con became more casual and familiar. At one appointment, he asked me to give him a review online, and I did. At the next appointment, he asked me if I knew of any child-friendly restaurants. I listed some that I could imagine fitting a pram into.

One Tuesday morning while I was at work, I received an email to my personal account from an unknown address. The subject line said, *It's your dentist James!* I froze. Why was Dr Con emailing me? He had never emailed me before. Had my last transaction bounced? No – that was a full month ago. How could Dr Con's receptionist take a full month to realise that my transaction had bounced? And why was the dentist chasing up that $250 personally? I clicked on the notification with the kind of apprehension you usually only feel in a dentist's chair.

Hi Sinead. it started, with a very ominous and aggressive use of a full-stop.

I hope you've been super well. My friends asked me for some fresh places to go to (bars) in the city, so I figured it would be best to ask you!

Appreciated in advance!

I stared at the email in shock. Did this mean that Dr Con had been talking to his friends about me? Did that mean that in some dentist group chat his friends had said, *Hey, what bar should we go to?* and then Dr Con had said, *I'll ask that patient who works at the culture website*, and then they said, *The one who dribbles and who started crying that time?* and he said, *Yes, that one …?*

If I ignored this email – which I am always inclined to do when anything uncomfortable is asked of me – would that make it awkward when I went back in five months? Would Dr Con use the poker and not try to distract me from it? Would he charge me double? This person was in charge of my wellbeing at my most vulnerable moments – he was too powerful to offend.

I sent him back three suggestions of newly opened bars in the CBD, cringing as I typed. He immediately wrote back: *Thanks so much, Sinead! Also this line's always open to you, of course.*

I tried to imagine a scenario in which my only course of action would be emailing my dentist. I wouldn't want to waste his time.

Well, I guess it's time to buy a dress

Like most close female friends, Imogen and I frequently texted, Facebook messaged and emailed during the workday. In our early twenties, this was mostly to comfort each other about the microaggressions we'd been dealt by our mostly male bosses – bosses who wanted to talk at length about what it felt like when *Bleach* came out but did not like discussing pay parity. In our late twenties, at times we would send a string of ten or fifteen messages trying to schedule a dinner, only to conclude that a breakfast between 7.15am and 8.30am in three weeks' time was the only window in which we were both free. We had met on the first day of Year Seven, when our homeroom teacher made her stand in front of the class and explain that she was vision impaired. We hadn't even gotten our class timetables yet or worked out how to open our lockers.

'That was weird,' I said as she sat down next to me.

'Yeah,' she said. We've been best friends ever since.

She was the sort of person to whom I would confess the worst and most embarrassing stuff I did, because purposely debasing ourselves for each other's amusement was part of the game.

Hey want to hear something funny, Imogen texted me one Friday afternoon, while I was sitting at my desk editing urgent ad copy.

Always, I texted back immediately.

Imogen, in between soothing my existential ennui, often told very funny stories. Many of these stories related to her unpredictably explosive bowels. I don't recall her being diagnosed with anything specifically bowel-related, but it was common knowledge among our friends and families that when it came to shitting, Imogen's butt had a mind of its own. Diet did not seem to alter this fact, nor sheer force of will. When her insides decided it was time to evacuate her body, there was often no warning or reason for it. It was sort of like at the end of *Point Break* when Patrick Swayze walks away from the shore and into the ocean, except the shore was Imogen's intestines and the sea was whatever receptacle was closest and Patrick Swayze was a load of diarrhoea.

One time, when she was on a romantic holiday in Berlin with a partner – staying in a hostel that was so spotlessly white-surfaced and clinically clean that it could have doubled as a Swiss mental institution – she shat the bed in her sleep. It transpired that she had contracted gastro from her family when they saw her off at the airport, the gastro germs percolating in her guts during the flights to Europe then releasing when she arrived at her pristine destination. It was her partner who discovered this situation as Imogen slept soundly in their shared white-linen sheets.

Another time, Imogen was emptying the dishwasher while talking to her boyfriend, and as she squatted down to retrieve a plate, she somehow spontaneously did a shit at such a velocity that it burst through her tracksuit pants and splattered onto the floor. She had not been sick or eaten anything strange that day. She said that she hadn't even felt it coming until it was too late. It was almost impressive. She had texted me about it immediately.

This time, though, Imogen wasn't texting about defecating on the kitchen floor. She wasn't texting about defecating at all. *I think I'm coming around to the whole marriage thing, hey,* she wrote, then sending a second text straight away: *I've decided I want to have a love party with John one day, but want to have a kid soon either way.*

I stared at the text. It suddenly felt like my bones were made of lead and my blood made of mercury. The text slid out of focus, and it felt like my eyes were somehow retracting inside my head. I suddenly felt inexplicably, overwhelmingly sad, like I had unwittingly taken the greatest MDMA of all time the night before and was now suffering from the steepest comedown in all of human and drug history.

She sent a third text: *Isn't that funny?*

I couldn't wait too long to reply, because she would know something was up. *OMG* I wrote back, repeating that same text five times in a row. I knew this was good. I knew this wasn't a surprise. I knew I should be happy for her. John had seen her take a shit on their kitchen floor and he still saw her as marriage material.

Why am I not happy? I asked myself for the rest of the afternoon. I sleepwalked through my work that day and was distracted when meeting other friends that night at the pub. *Didn't I know this was on the cards?*

I thought back to a commitment ceremony Imogen and I had attended a few months before, in which she confessed that maybe marriage wasn't the demon hell prison we'd always assumed it was. 'Now that gay people can get married it's more a possibility, ya know?' she had said, while we sculled our standard one water to every four sparkling wines. Hadn't I felt pleased for her then? Curious about what would come from this change of heart? Was I the type of person who was only glad of her friends' potential happiness when it was theoretical?

I had seen many movies about women in romantic, all-encompassing friendships who were suddenly split when one of them entered a new life stage. The other woman, who was just living the same way she always had, would feel abandoned and judged as juvenile. In small ways I had related to Frances Ha's confusion when her best friend's boyfriend's friends knew more about her best friend's life than she did. I understood Annie in

Bridesmaids feeling threatened that her newly engaged best friend, Lillian, had a new, mature and more sophisticated friend. That pressure, that belief that we're meant to act in certain prescribed ways during certain periods of our lives, creeps up on you in such dramatic ways that it almost makes you want to act even *more* like a savage, running drunk through the streets to the house party of a photographer friend you sort of knew from back in the day, wasting time and boasting about the lack of a house and kids to tie you down. What a cliché I was.

The thing these movies don't always explain is that you're not jealous because you would like someone to ask you to marry you. You're not jealous because you want a kid. At least, maybe some people feel that way, but I didn't. I was jealous because I realised that I had somehow convinced myself that I was the centre of someone's universe, and I wasn't. Imogen being married wouldn't mean that she would become too busy for forty-five-minute midweek breakfasts or too preoccupied to send me texts about shitting herself (maybe that would change if she had a kid, though I expected that the amount of 'shitting' texts would probably increase). But it meant that she was deliberately and very thoughtfully tying herself to another human being, and that human being was not me.

If this sounds very, 'Ah, are you in love with your best friend?' I understand. Everything was just so perfect that I didn't want things to change. Female friendships forged in early adolescence have a romance and intimacy to them that is hard to convey, and it's equally hard to convey how her thinking about marriage felt – illogically and dramatically – like a cosmic tie was being snipped. (Though I knew that if I even mentioned feeling left behind, she would enthusiastically attempt to make me feel like the most validated person who had ever drawn breath.) I hadn't even realised that I thought I should be her number one priority until she decided she might legally attach herself to someone else. And what *about* that – what did that mean for *my* relationship? My boyfriend and I had been together for a long time; we lived together. I knew I wanted to be with him in perpetuity. He was my best friend. Did the fact that we weren't having those conversations mean that we were just playing house? Did my lack of romantic ambition betray something broken in my skull? Did it mean something that we weren't thinking of our relationship in stages?

This feeling was completely new and yet strangely familiar. For so much of my twenties I had been fixated on having the correct tastes, searching for reassurance that I liked and did the right things. Now – with my best friend, who I had mirrored in so many ways since I was twelve, taking a different path – I was confronted with a game that transcended any pursuit of coolness. The new measure of worth was achieving the 'correct' life stage, and the new way I could be left behind was if I wasn't being an adult in the way that was suddenly being modelled all around me.

It wasn't the first time I'd had the feeling that I wasn't as grown up as I was meant to be. One lunchtime in Year Nine, my friends were gathered around discussing a big (and unsupervised) party we'd all be attending that weekend.

'I reckon I'm going to get four of those red Vodka Cruisers,' said my friend Beck, sitting on top of a desk and pushing down her school socks.

'Mum is going to get me UDLs,' said Imogen, as she stretched out in front of the heater.

The other girls started doing the maths of how many drinks they could get and whose mums or older siblings could provide them. I was in total shock. At lunch the day before, we had been discussing whether Millsy would win *Australian Idol*. Alcohol had never been mentioned before, and now everyone was acting like it was just something that we always did. My friend Steph fidgeted beside me. I found out later that she was feeling the same panic as me: the same fear that she had somehow missed a vital step towards adulthood. Did it happen when we were in the bathroom or something? She brought a six-pack of juice boxes to the party and made a joke out of it. I was given a single Smirnoff Double Black by a friend, got very red in the face while dancing to 'Hey Ya!' and was told to have some water by the only adult at the party.

For the past few years, Imogen had sometimes mentioned that she wanted to have kids – a fact that I always very callously brushed over, because I didn't want to think about it. I didn't want to think about it not just because it was another place I didn't want to follow her, or because it made me anxious that

I didn't want to do the 'right' things, but because if Imogen had a baby it would be deeply inconvenient for me and my social life. Our lives would change and it would be annoying. I decided to pretend it wasn't happening.

'The thing is, I just don't want it to change me,' Imogen said over a pub dinner one night. 'Nothing will have to change.'

We both ate our chips in silence for a few seconds.

'I mean, things *will* change,' I said, without being able to stop myself. 'Things will change because they will have to change.'

Imogen looked at me like I had stabbed her in the chest. 'Well, yes, I guess so,' she said quietly. I felt like a dick.

Only one of my close friends had had a baby, so the whole thing was still a novelty. I had met Tess while working at a youth media website, and we'd followed each other to another job because we thought that it would pay better (it did), that it would be easy (it wasn't) and that it would be funny (it was, at first).

She was the opposite of me in that she was good at everything: she played basketball, had hitchhiked in Argentina, had driven in a four-wheel drive across the Northern Territory and had admirable party stamina. When I hung out with Tess, I was louder and said ridiculous things. We would passionately discuss alternative ways of living (we both pretended we'd consider joining a commune when we turned thirty), debated books that we had read (she was the only person I knew who read as much as me) and unpacked the way our cultural context had impacted our identities (I once caught her at after-work drinks lecturing our 21-year-old co-worker at length about how September 11 had affected the millennial consciousness; he looked too scared to move).

When Tess got engaged, she asked me to be her bridesmaid on our lunch break at Guzman y Gomez and we both cried, then immediately googled *what does a bridesmaid do?* on our phones. At the last work party we both attended, we got drunk on free cocktails and each stole a wheel of cheese from the company's artisanal charcuterie table by stuffing them in bin bags and pretending they were rubbish. Two months later, she found out she was pregnant.

Tess approached her pregnancy as if it was the weirdest and funniest thing to have ever happened to a human body, which gave me permission to treat it that way, too. It occurred to me that nine months is the exact time it takes for a human brain to come to terms with the fact that a pregnancy results in a *human being* who is then part of the equation. By the time her son was born, I was elated in the way that a kid is when they know they're going to get a new toy. *This is my new best friend,* I posted on Instagram on the day that he was born. *All other friends go to hell.*

The next few months were the quietest in mine and Tess' friendship. Not because we didn't talk to each other – we chatted on Facebook almost every day, and I visited semi-frequently – but I didn't know what the rules were when your friend had a baby. I wasn't sure how to be helpful and didn't want to put the pressure on her to decide how I could *be* helpful. I couldn't help with the lack of sleep, or pain, and I had to stop myself from repeating, '*I can't believe you created a fucking person,*' after the first few weeks because I knew my awe was getting annoying. I googled early motherhood to get a sense of what she needed, but I had never felt more useless. Was it annoying when I visited? What was the correct amount of time to stay? Should I avoid talking about gigs I had been to or books I had read, in case it upset her? Is it more boring for *her* if we only talk about the baby? Like I had suddenly cast her as 'Mum' and erased her previous identity?

When one of your best mates has a baby, it can lead you to judge yourself in a really weird way. Suddenly the idea of complaining to her about something nasty someone said at work or a joke you saw on Twitter seems insignificant. Talking about the despair I felt not being able to fit into a certain pair of jeans, or my favourite bits of *John Wick 3* seemed insensitive. Writing a book about self-improvement while Tess was at home trying to keep a human being alive seemed fucking juvenile. When the baby arrived, I was cast in a new and largely unflattering light, like I was a packet of ham sitting on a shelf in the Coles deli section. She was a married woman with a son and I was still in the cheese-stealing stage of my life.

The baby is a year old now. Tess has eased into a rhythm – as much as you can have a rhythm with a little nonsense machine who is constantly attempting to pull large and unstable pieces of furniture on top of himself and literally needs your boobs to survive. I'm still worried that I'm not being the perfect friend to her, but am trying to quash that hyperactive, hysterical attempt to anticipate her needs, as if it'll say something definitively terrible about my soul if I ever get it wrong. The other week I went over for an afternoon beer with the intention of staying for an hour just to give myself a break from writing. I ended up staying for dinner time, then bath time, then adult dinner time, and by 11pm we were dancing to The Presets in her kitchen while the baby snoozed in the other room. I didn't feel guilty about it.

My friend Louise has since gotten engaged. I've already started bossing her around trying to get her to start planning the wedding. Steph got engaged, too – she's moving overseas with her partner, to teach in Vietnam. Recently, Imogen and John made an offer on a house.

'I want to tell you exactly how all this stuff works,' Imogen said during one of our breakfasts (7.35am – 8.46am), her mouth full of scrambled egg and toast.

'It's so boring, I can't get that stuff to stick in my head,' I said, my mouth full of peanut-butter toast.

'No, *that's what they want you to think*!' Imogen hissed, as if we were surrounded by house-buying baby boomers who would hear us educating ourselves on the property market and murder us where we sat.

After we left each other and went to work, we chatted online all day (Imogen had set up a separate Slack channel called 'Friendship'). She'd read a few articles about motherhood and sent them to me to discuss. We both got mad at the idea of people policing pregnant bodies, raging about the patriarchy, swearing more than was necessary because we were excited to be having a conversation about babies where we were on the same side. 'Maybe next year is the year,' she said.

At about 6pm, I received a photo of Imogen and John smiling goofy smiles. *We got the house and thirty years of mortgage, love you*, her following text said. I yelped and showed my colleagues.

OMG, I texted back, and I meant it in a good way.

What if

What if instead of being scared of fucking up all the time, I decided that I only needed to be 80 per cent good, that I didn't have to wait for someone to tell me I'm good and could trust that I am, and that even aiming for that amount of good is too much? That maybe we're all 50 per cent to 70 per cent good, actually? And that might be okay? In the scheme of it all?

    Huh

    Huh

    Huh

tl;dr

You know the feeling that you could be a bit cooler, a bit warmer, a bit easier to get along with, a bit more lovable, get the haircut that suits your face, always have your nails done and be able to do maths in your head?

Maybe everyone sort of feels like that, but some people are just better at hiding it. The people who don't might just be jerks.

This book is about that feeling that something is fundamentally wrong with you, but you can't figure out what so you run in circles and whip your head around quickly as if you can identify it on sight. It's sort of what I imagine dogs feel like on airplanes – like something really bad is happening in the very air around them, and they don't know if maybe they should just get used to this new, worse mode of living – but then eventually the plane lands. You'll feel like you're on a plane again eventually, but you'll understand it a bit better next time. You're a smart dog.

It's about realising that maybe there is no perfect version of yourself and it's actually all about the shitty version of yourself: the self with yellow teeth and weak knees, and a love of trashy TV shows and music that was fashionable fifteen years ago; the self who sometimes says mean stuff but mostly only does that by accident. It's about realising that acting like that better version of yourself all the time is very tiring indeed.

It's about realising that the 'catastrophe of your personality' is the best bit, but you'll have to keep reminding yourself of that because it's not anyone else's job.

It's about wishing that when you opened this book it could play a song like musical greeting cards do, but instead of 'Happy Birthday' it would play 'The Song That Doesn't End' by Lamb Chop, but maybe that idea is too future.

It's about figuring out that even the act of writing a book, and forcing yourself to believe that people will want to spend time with you for the length of the book, is like blowing little wisps of hope into the breeze as if they were bits of a dandelion.

It's about realising that you can beat yourself up about something you did five years ago – or twenty years ago – but that was a different version of yourself and you have permission to change. You're not chained to your old personality or old opinions. You can get better, but you don't have to be perfect. Honestly, that sanctimonious level of good is the reason why *The Brady Bunch* parents were so irritating. Their neighbours probably hated them. Alice was likely slowly poisoning them the whole time.

It's about knowing that you will never know how to do a cat's eye, but you can just pay someone to do one if it's a life-and-death situation.

It's about realising that you don't have to be perfect to be loved. When you stuff up, they won't all abandon you. It's about cracking your ribs open and showing strangers your real weird, abnormally shaped heart and wondering if they possess real weird, abnormally shaped hearts, too.

It's about figuring out that the things that people like about you – and the things that you kind of like about yourself – are the things with rough edges, so you don't have to put so much energy into smoothing yourself out. You start to realise that maybe everyone feels a bit defective, even if they appear cool and wise.

It's about feeling like a fraud writing a book at all, because self-deprecating books can be very annoying and it's not like your perspective hasn't been represented before, but you're not actually fixing anything by being a martyr, you're just being a real wuss. Your guilt and your shame is not radical. You can control how many times you secretly re-watch *A Little Princess*, but you can't control what people think about you.

It's about remembering the time you were called a 'try-hard' in 1999 and laughing so much when you tell your boyfriend the story that you decide to write a whole book about it. Sucked in, I guess.

Acknowledgments

First of all, if you have made it this far, thank you for sticking with this book. I still find it shocking that people I've never even met could be reading this. I wrote stories every Saturday for a year and then, *plonk!* a book came out and now you are holding it. I hope it has kept you company in lunch breaks and when you were waiting for a friend to turn up at the bar and right before bed, when you needed to distract yourself from sending a text that could ruin your life. I'm so grateful that you read it.

I couldn't have written a book without having someone email me 'where is the book' so thank you Danielle Binks for being the most patient agent to ever exist. I'm so glad that you trusted I could write something larger than 'Pacey Witter destroyed my life, here's how'. Thank you too to Jacinta de Mase for seeing that talk and seeing something in me that I did not.

Thank you to Ruby Asby-Orr at Affirm Press for being so thoughtful, making me sound so much better and saying 'You're freaking out about nothing' about twenty times during this process. Thank you also to Martin Hughes for liking the book so much and saying that it was a bright spark in a bad week. I don't think you realise how important that was for me to hear.

Now, the big guns: thank you Deirdre, Johnny, Monica and Ciarán for being so supportive of me, reminding me to go easier on myself and giving me permission to tell everyone our stories. Mama and Dada, thanks for working so hard to send me to nice schools, buying me notebooks to write in and not minding that I wanted to write frivolous stories for a living (it's still not a living, oops). Monc and Ciri, you're the best siblings anyone could ever have and the people I like hanging out with best, even if you're both dumb-tall and likely born of giraffes. It'll be super embarrassing when everyone finds out that all four of you are funnier than I am, but guess what? You'll have to get a book deal for them to figure it out. In this economy? Good luck, losers. I'm so proud to be part of this family. Thank you also to my cousins, who are my favourite storytellers and who were probably my first readers. (Remember that newspaper Clare got us to do?)

There are a few people who I owe a million emotional bucks to. Thank you Bhakthi for being my reader and the person who is able to discern when I think a my writing is rubbish because I'm wired to think *everything* is rubbish, and when I think it's rubbish because it actually *is* rubbish. I'm so glad and so lucky that I met you. Thank you Brodie for, when I said, 'How do other writers write books that are not annoying?!' reminding me that they probably are annoying, I just have more empathy for them than I do for myself. Likewise to Taryn, who would repeat 'you can't control that!' seventy to eighty times a month and who would quite literally laugh in my face when I said something melodramatic about chucking it all in. Thank you Anna, Sezzy, Nicole and Ilya for still being my friends even when I have been boring and stayed home to write stories about the Titanic.

Thanks to Nat from Beatrix for keeping me in roulades, pies, cookies, slices, scrolls and layer cakes on Saturday mornings, because no one ever wrote anything interesting while eating muesli.

Thank you to Sophie Black, Penny Modra, Ben Birchall, Tam Zimet, Nayuka Gorrie and Max Olijnyk for encouraging me to write a book at various restless points in my life (even if you can't remember, I remember). Thank you to Bridie and Svetlana at *The Guardian* for commissioning me to write about funny things I had seen and felt, and for letting me build on some of those pieces and publish them in this collection.

Thank you to Brigid: not only could I not have written a book without you, I am not sure I could have survived adolescence or my twenties without you. Dramatic! It feels stupid to try to sum up how much you mean to me, because imagining my life without you is like saying, 'Wouldn't it be weird if you woke up one morning and there was suddenly no sky? Or our feet were giant doughnuts?' It's just a hard concept to wrap your head around. Thank you for letting me tell our stories. (And thank you to Jess, the third Amigo in many of these stories – I miss you and I think you should stop travelling the world and come home now please!)

Thank you to the drug valium and to Medicare.

Most of all to my best friend, Andy, who makes the best dinners, has the best laugh, is exceedingly generous and patient with me and who is the best person I've ever met.